The Simplified Handbook on Wix Website Builder and Development for Pros and Beginners:

Step-by-Step Instructions for Building and Optimizing Websites with Wix Tools

Deven Porter

Table of Contents

Overview

In a world where every business, personal project, or creative endeavor needs an online presence, having a website isn't just a luxury; it's a necessity. But with countless platforms offering various ways to build a website, where does one begin? The task of creating a website can feel like a daunting challenge, especially when you're not a tech expert or when you have no prior knowledge of web development. The overwhelming variety of tools and jargon can discourage you before you even start. You may ask yourself, "How can I possibly build something that stands out, represents me, or drives my business forward?" The truth is, creating a beautiful, functional, and professional website is within your reach. And with the right guidance, you can do it.

Welcome to "The Simplified Handbook on Wix Website Builder and Development for Pros and Beginners." This book is your roadmap, your guide, and your unwavering support system on the journey to building a site that not only looks good but also performs at its best. Whether you are just starting or have some experience under your belt, you've come to the right place. With a step-by-step approach, this book will lead you through the entire process of designing, developing, and maintaining a site that serves your goals and needs.

Imagine waking up one morning, excited to share your thoughts with the world or launch your business in a way that draws customers in. The first step? Having a platform where your ideas come to life. With Wix, the possibilities are endless. It's a platform that is not just for tech experts but for anyone with a vision—a platform that empowers creators, business owners, and individuals alike to take their dreams online. But how do you harness the full potential of Wix? That's exactly what this book is here to help you with.

For those of you who may be beginners, the journey might feel overwhelming. You may feel like you're stepping into a world of complicated design software, techy jargon, and settings that seem confusing. But it doesn't have to be that way. This book takes away the complexity and simplifies the process. We will go through each step, one by one, making sure you understand every concept and are comfortable with every tool before moving forward. You'll soon realize that building your site isn't as hard as you thought, and you don't need to be a computer expert to create something that reflects your personality, business, or brand.

As we dive deeper into Wix's powerful tools, you will discover how easy it is to create a stunning site, even without any prior experience. From choosing the right template to customizing the smallest details, this book will empower you to build a website that's uniquely yours. The drag-and-drop editor in Wix is designed with simplicity in mind, allowing anyone, from a complete novice to an experienced pro, to make their website look professional and feel personal.

But what about the advanced users? For those of you who have already dabbled in website creation or web development, you may be seeking more than just the basics. You want control, flexibility, and the ability to create a truly unique experience for your visitors. Don't worry; we've got you covered. In this book, we'll explore the advanced features of Wix—tools like Velo, Wix's developer platform, which gives you the ability to write custom code and create dynamic, database-driven websites. You'll learn how to take your site from basic to brilliant, unlocking the full potential of Wix as a development platform.

No matter your skill level, this book will take you through each stage of building a website—from designing the perfect layout and choosing the right elements to optimizing your site for search engines and mobile devices. You'll learn about SEO, mobile responsiveness, performance optimization, and much more. And as you work your way through the content, you'll notice something truly magical happening: not only are you learning how to build a website, but you're also gaining the confidence and skills needed to handle your site's growth over time.

This book isn't just about teaching you how to build a website; it's about helping you build a foundation for your online future. It's about making sure that your website is more than just a page on the internet—it's a powerful tool that works for you. Whether your website is for personal expression, your small business, or a large-scale e-commerce store, the tools and techniques you'll learn in this book will help you every step of the way.

Perhaps, you've tried building a website before and found the experience frustrating. Maybe you've felt lost in the technicalities of coding, design, or SEO. Or perhaps you've felt stuck, unable to make your site look or function the way you wanted it to. If this sounds familiar, this book is here to help you break free from those roadblocks. We'll show you how to create a site that you can be proud of—one that is visually stunning, user-friendly, and optimized for success.

Building a website with Wix isn't just about placing images and text on a page. It's about crafting an experience that resonates with your visitors, a space that speaks to your audience, and encourages engagement. In this book, you'll find practical tips for creating a cohesive, visually appealing design, as well as techniques for keeping your content fresh and up-to-date. You'll also learn how to make your website interactive and engaging, with tools that allow your visitors to connect with you, make purchases, or learn more about your business or brand.

But beyond the tools and techniques, this book is about something more profound: empowering you to take control of your digital future. The ability to create your website opens up endless possibilities. Imagine how freeing it will feel to have complete control over your online presence. Imagine the pride you'll feel when you look at your site and know you built it yourself. And the best part is, you're not doing it alone. With every page you turn, we're right there with you, providing guidance and support as you navigate the world of Wix website creation.

As you read on, remember that this isn't just a book about Wix; it's a book about you- your journey, your dreams, and your business. Whether you're launching a blog, setting up an online store, or simply building a portfolio, this book will give you the tools, knowledge, and encouragement to succeed. It will show you how to make the most of Wix's features while keeping the process fun, creative, and stress-free.

By the time you finish this book, you won't just know how to build a website; you'll have created a platform that showcases your talents, helps you reach your goals, and sets you up for success in the digital world. So, take a deep breath and prepare yourself for a transformative journey. The path to building your dream website starts here, and we'll be with you every step of the way.

Introduction

In today's digital world, the need for an online presence has never been more crucial. Whether you are a small business owner looking to reach a broader audience, a creative individual wanting to showcase your portfolio, or someone with a passion project that you want to share with the world, a website is often the first point of interaction with your audience. But, the process of creating a website can feel like an insurmountable task, especially when you're unsure where to begin. Do you need to hire a developer? Do you have to learn complicated code? Is there a way to create a website without it costing an arm and a leg?

This book, *The Simplified Handbook on Wix Website Builder and Development for Pros and Beginners*, is designed to answer these questions and guide you through every step of the website creation process. Whether you are a complete beginner with no technical knowledge or an experienced professional looking to refine your web development skills, this guide will equip you with the tools and knowledge necessary to build a stunning, functional, and user-friendly website.

Throughout this book, we will explore Wix, a powerful and intuitive website builder that makes the process of creating a website accessible to everyone. No matter your level of expertise, you will learn how to harness the full potential of Wix to create a website that reflects your vision, your brand, and your unique voice.

Wix is a platform that has revolutionized the world of web design by offering an easy-to-use drag-and-drop interface, a variety of customizable templates, and a host of powerful tools that can cater to the needs of both beginners and professionals alike. But it's not just about creating a website; it's about making sure that your website not only looks great but also functions seamlessly, attracts visitors, and achieves your goals. With this book, you will master both the basics and advanced features of Wix, so you can create a website that serves your needs and grows with you over time.

The Book's Purpose and Audience (Pros and Beginners)

This book is designed for a diverse audience, including newcomers to the world of web development and experienced professionals who want to improve their skills. Whether you have never touched a website builder before or already have a website but want to take it to the next level, this guide will provide you with the knowledge, skills, and tools necessary to succeed.

For **beginners**, the idea of building a website can be overwhelming. You may be unfamiliar with web design terminology, or perhaps you've tried to build a website in the past only to find the process frustrating and confusing. This book will help you break through those barriers. We will guide you through the process of selecting a template, customizing it to suit your needs, and adding the necessary functionality to make your website work for you. With easy-to-follow instructions and clear, practical examples, you will gain the confidence to create a website that is both visually appealing and functional.

For **professionals**, you may already have some experience with Wix or other website-building platforms. However, you might be seeking more advanced features and customizations that will allow you to create truly unique websites. Whether it's adding custom code, working with dynamic databases, or using Wix's powerful developer tools, this book will delve into the more technical aspects of Wix to ensure that you can fully unlock the platform's potential. We'll explore how to take your website from basic to brilliant, incorporating advanced features and design elements that will give your site the competitive edge it needs to stand out in a crowded digital world.

No matter where you fall on the spectrum of expertise, this book is here to ensure that you fully understand Wix and its capabilities. We'll start with the basics, gradually moving into more advanced topics, ensuring that both beginners and pros can keep up and learn something valuable along the way.

Brief Introduction to Wix as a Platform

Wix is a cloud-based website-building platform that has become one of the most popular and user-friendly options for creating websites. Whether you're an individual looking to build a personal blog or a business owner looking to create a professional website, Wix offers an extensive array of features to help you bring your ideas to life. One of the reasons Wix has gained such popularity is that it democratizes web design, making it accessible to people who have no prior experience with coding or design.

At the heart of Wix is its **drag-and-drop editor**, which allows users to build websites visually. Instead of having to code HTML, CSS, or JavaScript, you can select elements like text boxes, images, videos, buttons, and forms, and place them exactly where you want them on the page. This makes the process incredibly intuitive and easy, even for those who have never touched a website builder before.

Wix offers a wide variety of **templates**, each designed for different types of websites. Whether you're looking to build an e-commerce store, a portfolio, a blog, or a business website, you'll find a template that fits your needs. These templates are fully customizable, so you can tweak every detail to make sure your site is unique and reflects your personal or brand identity.

But what truly sets Wix apart is the breadth of features it offers. In addition to the basic tools for website creation, Wix provides powerful **SEO tools**, **mobile optimization**, **e-commerce capabilities**, **blogging functionality**, and more. With Wix, you can not only build a website but also ensure that it is optimized for search engines, looks great on mobile devices, and is ready to handle online transactions.

For those with a more technical background or a desire to create a truly unique website, Wix offers **Velo** (formerly Corvid), its developer platform. This platform allows you to add custom code, interact with databases, and integrate third-party applications. This makes Wix a versatile platform that can grow with your needs, whether you're just starting or are looking to build a complex, feature-rich website.

Importance of Understanding Both Basic and Advanced Wix Tools

Wix offers a range of tools for both **beginners** and **advanced users**, and understanding how to use both is crucial to creating a truly outstanding website.

For **beginners**, it's important to master the basic tools first. The drag-and-drop editor, template customization, and simple design features will allow you to get started quickly and effectively. You'll learn how to create a professional-looking website without needing to learn any complex coding or design principles. These basic tools provide an excellent foundation for website creation, and they can take you a long way in building a simple website that meets your needs.

However, as you grow and become more comfortable with the platform, you'll want to take your skills to the next level by exploring Wix's **advanced tools**. For example, Wix allows you to add custom code through Velo, create dynamic pages with databases, and integrate your website with other third-party applications. These advanced features give you greater flexibility and control over your website, allowing you to build highly customized and sophisticated websites.

Understanding both the basic and advanced tools is essential for maximizing Wix's potential. The basic tools will allow you to get started and create a functional website quickly, while the advanced tools will provide the power and flexibility you need to create truly unique and complex websites. As you progress through this book, you'll see how these two sets of tools complement each other and how combining them can help you create a website that not only looks great but also works for your specific needs and goals.

What to Expect in This Book: A Comprehensive Guide from Setup to Advanced Features

This book is designed to provide you with a comprehensive, step-by-step guide to Wix, from the very basics of setting up your account to the advanced features that can take your website to the next level. We will cover every aspect of website creation, ensuring that you have the knowledge and skills necessary to build a website that meets your personal or professional needs.

In the first part of the book, we'll focus on the **fundamentals**—how to sign up for Wix, choose a template, and begin customizing your website. You'll learn how to add and arrange elements on your pages, change your site's layout, and create a user-friendly experience for your visitors. This section will be perfect for beginners who need a strong foundation before diving into more complex topics.

As we move forward, we will delve into **advanced features**, including how to integrate Wix's Velo developer tools, create dynamic pages that automatically update with new content, and build a custom database for your website. These advanced features are ideal for those who want to take full control of their website and create something unique.

Along the way, we will also cover topics such as **SEO optimization**, **mobile responsiveness**, and **site performance**—all of which are essential to ensuring that your website is visible, fast, and accessible to users on all devices.

Finally, this book will provide you with practical tips for **maintaining and updating your website** and strategies for growing your online presence over time. You'll learn how to monitor your website's performance, track visitors using Google Analytics, and make updates as your site evolves.

By the end of this book, you'll be able to confidently create, manage, and optimize a Wix website that meets your goals, whether you're just starting or are looking to refine your existing site. The knowledge and skills you gain here will empower you to take control of your online presence and create a website that stands out in a crowded digital world.

This book is more than just a guide to Wix—it's a roadmap to your success in the digital landscape.

Whether you are looking to build a personal blog, start an e-commerce store, or showcase your creative work, this book will help you unlock the full potential of Wix and give you the tools you need to succeed.

Chapter 1: Getting Started with Wix

The world of web development has evolved significantly in the past few years. Gone are the days when creating a website meant hiring expensive developers or learning complicated code. With the advent of user-friendly website builders like Wix, anyone with a computer and an internet connection can now create a professional-looking website, no matter their level of experience. Wix has been at the forefront of this revolution, offering a platform that is accessible, flexible, and packed with tools to help users design and develop websites easily.

This chapter will walk you through the basics of getting started with Wix. We will break down the platform's functionality, explain how its drag-and-drop interface works, explore the different plans available, and give you a comprehensive understanding of the Wix dashboard—an essential tool that will be your hub for managing your website. Whether you're a complete beginner or someone with a bit of experience in web design, this chapter will give you the foundation you need to start building your Wix website.

What is Wix? An Introduction to the Platform

Wix is a cloud-based website-building platform that has taken the world by storm. It offers a simple yet powerful way to create websites without needing any prior experience with coding or design. Founded in 2006, Wix has grown to become one of the most popular website builders available today, with millions of users around the world. It allows individuals and businesses to create anything from a basic portfolio or blog to a fully functional e-commerce store.

What makes Wix stand out is its **intuitive drag-and-drop interface**, which allows users to create websites visually, without writing a single line of code. Unlike traditional web development, where you need to understand HTML, CSS, and JavaScript, Wix simplifies the process by providing an interface where you can place elements exactly where you want them. You select the components—such as text boxes, images, videos, buttons, and more—and drag them into place. Wix will handle the back-end technicalities, including responsiveness, compatibility, and optimization.

One of the main reasons Wix has become such a popular platform is its versatility. It caters to a broad spectrum of users, from complete beginners to experienced professionals who need advanced customization options. Whether you're an artist, a photographer, a small business owner, or someone who wants to create a personal blog, Wix has the tools and resources to help you bring your vision to life. It offers a wide selection of pre-designed templates, a large app marketplace, and various integrations that allow you to extend the functionality of your site.

How Wix Works: A Simple Explanation of Its Drag-and-Drop Interface

The true beauty of Wix lies in its **drag-and-drop editor**, which is designed to make website creation accessible to everyone, regardless of their technical skills. With Wix's drag-and-drop system, you don't need to worry about complex layouts, code, or formatting issues. Instead, you can focus on the design, layout, and content of your site, while Wix takes care of the technical side.

When you first log into Wix, you'll be presented with a blank canvas or a pre-designed template. The drag-and-drop editor allows you to add various elements to your pages easily. These elements include text boxes, images, videos, buttons, contact forms, and much more. To add an element, all you have to do is drag it from the sidebar and drop it into the desired spot on your page. You can resize, reposition, and customize these elements with ease.

Each element comes with its own set of editing options, allowing you to adjust fonts, colors, borders, and alignment. For instance, if you're adding a text box, you can change the font, size, color, and style to match the theme of your site. Similarly, when you add an image, you can choose the size and positioning, and you can even add special effects such as filters, shadows, and animations.

What sets Wix's drag-and-drop editor apart from others is its **intuitive user interface**. The system works in real-time, which means that you can see the changes you make instantly. It's a highly interactive experience that allows you to fine-tune every detail of your website with ease. Whether you're adjusting the size of an image or moving a button to a different spot on the page, Wix's drag-and-drop editor makes these changes feel natural and effortless.

In addition to basic elements, Wix also allows you to add **dynamic features** like contact forms, booking systems, social media integrations, and e-commerce tools with just a few clicks. The platform is designed to handle the technical complexities for you, so all you need to focus on is designing a site that reflects your unique style or business identity.

The Difference Between Wix Free Plan and Premium Plans

One of the first decisions you'll face when setting up your Wix website is whether to use the **Free Plan** or upgrade to one of Wix's **Premium Plans**. The Free Plan offers a basic, entry-level option for creating and publishing a website, but it comes with several limitations. On the other hand, the Premium Plans unlock more advanced features and offer greater flexibility, making them a better option for businesses, professionals, or anyone who wants to take their website to the next level. Let's take a look at the differences between these plans:

Wix Free Plan

The **Free Plan** is ideal for beginners who are just testing out the platform or those who don't need advanced features. With the Free Plan, you can build and publish a website without any financial commitment. However, there are some key limitations:

- **Wix Ads**: Your site will display Wix advertisements, which can make your website appear less professional.

- **Limited Storage and Bandwidth**: You'll have limited storage space (500MB) and capacity (500MB), which can affect the performance of your website, especially if you're hosting large media files or expecting heavy traffic.

- **Wix Subdomain**: Your website will be hosted on a Wix subdomain (e.g., username.wixsite.com/sitename) rather than your custom domain name. This can make your website appear less credible or harder to find.

- **No E-commerce Features**: The Free Plan does not support online store functionality. If you want to sell products or services online, you'll need to upgrade to a Premium Plan.

Wix Premium Plans

Wix offers several Premium Plans, each designed to meet different needs. These plans unlock a range of features and enhancements, such as:

- **Custom Domain**: With a Premium Plan, you can connect your domain name (e.g., www.yoursite.com), which makes your site appear more professional and helps with branding.

- **No Ads**: Wix Ads are removed, providing a cleaner, more polished user experience.

- **Increased Storage and Bandwidth**: Premium Plans come with more storage space (starting at 3GB) and bandwidth (starting at 2GB), which is especially useful for larger websites with more content.

- **E-commerce Capabilities**: If you want to create an online store, Wix's Premium Plans include features for selling products, managing payments, and integrating with shipping carriers.

- **Advanced Features**: Premium Plans provide access to advanced tools such as Google

Analytics, SEO tools, and additional apps from the Wix App Market.

The pricing for Wix's Premium Plans varies depending on the features you need and the level of support required. The Combo Plan may suffice for small personal websites, but for businesses or larger websites, you may want to consider the **Business Basic** or **Unlimited Plan**, which offer more storage, bandwidth, and enhanced e-commerce capabilities.

Ultimately, the choice between the Free Plan and a Premium Plan depends on your specific needs. If you're creating a personal site or experimenting with the platform, the Free Plan is a good starting point. However, if you're serious about building a professional or business website, upgrading to a Premium Plan will give you the flexibility and features you need to succeed.

Setting Up a Wix Account and Selecting the Right Plan for Your Needs

Getting started with Wix is easy. Here's a step-by-step guide to setting up your account and selecting the right plan:

1. **Sign Up for Wix**: Visit the Wix website and click on the "Start Now" button. You'll be prompted to sign up for an account using either your email address or through a Google or Facebook account.

2. **Choose Your Plan**: After signing up, you'll be taken to the Wix dashboard, where you can choose the plan that best suits your needs. As mentioned earlier, if you're starting, the Free Plan is a great option. However, if you're looking to create a more professional site with your domain, additional storage, and no ads, you'll want to select one of the Premium Plans.

3. **Pick a Template**: Once you've selected your plan, you can start creating your website. Wix offers a vast library of templates designed for different industries and purposes. Whether you're building a business site, a personal portfolio, or an online store, there is a template for you. You can either choose to start with a blank template or let Wix's AI-powered tool, Wix ADI (Artificial Design Intelligence), create a custom site for you based on your preferences.

4. **Customize Your Site**: Once you've selected your template, you can begin customizing it using Wix's drag-and-drop editor. You can change the layout, add elements, and adjust the design to fit your unique vision.

5. **Connect Your Domain (Optional)**: If you've opted for a Premium Plan, you can now connect your custom domain name. You can either purchase a new domain through Wix or use an existing one.

6. **Publish Your Site**: After you've finished customizing your site, it's time to publish. Click the "Publish" button in the editor, and your website will be live for the world to see.

Exploring the Wix Dashboard: Key Features and Settings

The **Wix Dashboard** is your central hub for managing your website. Once you've signed up for Wix and logged into your account, you'll be taken to the dashboard, where you can access all the settings and features needed to build and manage your site. Here are some key features of the Wix Dashboard:

- **Site Overview**: The dashboard provides a quick overview of your site's performance, including traffic, sales (for e-commerce sites), and other key metrics.

- **Site Settings**: Here, you can adjust various site settings, including SEO settings, domain management, and social media integrations.

- **Editor**: This is where you'll spend most of your time. Clicking on "Edit Site" will open the drag-and-drop editor, allowing you to customize the layout, design, and content of your website.

- **Apps**: The Wix App Market is where you can browse and install third-party apps that add additional functionality to your site, such as chatbots, booking systems, and email marketing tools.

- **Billing and Subscriptions**: In this section, you can manage your subscription plan, upgrade or downgrade your plan, and manage billing details.

The Wix Dashboard is a user-friendly interface designed to simplify website management. Whether you're tweaking the design, analyzing site traffic, or managing your domain, everything you need is right at your fingertips.

This chapter has provided you with a solid foundation for understanding how Wix works, the differences between its Free and Premium plans, and how to set up your account and start building your website. In the next chapter, we'll dive deeper into Wix's templates and design tools, allowing you to begin crafting your site. Whether you're a complete beginner or an experienced web designer, Wix's intuitive platform and powerful features will make building your website a rewarding experience.

Chapter 2: Understanding Wix Templates

One of the most exciting aspects of using Wix to build your website is the vast array of pre-designed templates available to you. Whether you're creating a personal blog, launching a business, or showcasing your artistic portfolio, Wix's templates offer you a great starting point to build a site that matches your style and goals. Templates provide a pre-built structure that you can easily modify to suit your needs, saving you hours of design work. However, with so many options to choose from, it can sometimes feel overwhelming to decide which template is right for your project.

In this chapter, we'll explore how to choose the best template for your site, filter templates based on your industry or purpose, customize a template using Wix's built-in tools, and take things to the next level with advanced customization using Wix's developer platform, **Velo** (formerly Corvid by Wix). Whether you are a complete beginner or someone with a bit more experience, this chapter will guide you through the process of selecting and modifying templates to create a site that's uniquely yours.

Choosing the Right Template for Your Site

The first step in building your website on Wix is to choose a template that suits your site's purpose. Wix offers an extensive library of templates designed for various industries, including e-commerce, business, portfolios, blogs, events, restaurants, and more. Each template is designed for a specific type of website, so selecting the right one can help you avoid the need for extensive reworking later on.

When choosing a template, there are several key factors to keep in mind:

- **Industry and Purpose**: Different industries require different types of designs. A portfolio site for an artist will look very different from an e-commerce store for a retail business. Understanding your site's purpose will help you narrow down the options.

- **Design and Aesthetics**: Your website's look and feel are crucial. Choose a template that resonates with your personal or brand style. Wix templates are modern, responsive, and designed with user experience in mind, so it's important to select one that visually represents your website's purpose.

- **Functionality and Features**: Consider the features your website needs. If you're planning to sell products online, look for e-commerce templates that include integrated product galleries, shopping carts, and payment processing features. If you're building a personal blog or portfolio, focus on templates with clean layouts and blog capabilities.

Wix allows you to browse templates by category, making it easier to find the one that best suits your needs. Whether you're launching a blog, starting a business, or creating an online store, Wix has a template that fits your vision. Additionally, all Wix templates are fully customizable, meaning that you're not stuck with the exact design. You can modify colors, fonts, layouts, and more to suit your personal preferences.

Once you've selected a template, the next step is to customize it. This is where the real fun begins, as you can start tailoring the site to your brand's identity.

How to Filter Templates for Different Industries (e.g., Business, Portfolio, Blog, E-commerce)

Wix makes it incredibly easy to filter templates based on the type of website you're building. When you log into your Wix account and choose to create a new site, you'll be prompted to answer a few questions about the type of site you want to build. This will help Wix recommend templates that are best suited for your needs.

Here's a closer look at how to filter templates based on different industries:

Business Websites

If you're building a business website, whether it's for a small business, a corporate website, or a consultancy, Wix offers a wide variety of professional and clean templates. Wix templates for business websites typically feature:

- A clear call to action (CTA), such as a "Contact Us" or "Get Started" button.

- Space for showcasing services, products, and testimonials.

- Contact forms and integration with Google Maps for easy communication and location services.

To find business templates, use the filter in the template gallery to search for **business** or **corporate** sites. You can further refine your search to focus on specific industries, such as **law**, **real estate**, or **consulting**, ensuring that your template matches your niche.

Portfolio Websites

A portfolio website is essential for creative professionals who want to showcase their work, whether they are photographers, graphic designers, illustrators, or writers. Wix offers a large selection of stylish, image-driven portfolio templates that help highlight your best work. These templates typically include:

- Grid-based layouts to showcase your portfolio pieces.

- High-quality image spaces with options for full-screen displays.

- Sections for an "About Me" page and your professional background.

Suppose you're creating a portfolio; filter for **portfolio** templates in the Wix template gallery. You can also refine your search further by selecting categories like **photography**, **graphic design**, or **artistic portfolios** to find a template that suits your specific needs.

Blog Websites

Blogs are a fantastic way to share your thoughts, ideas, or expertise with the world. Wix provides a variety of customizable blog templates that focus on readability, ease of use, and functionality. These templates often feature:

- A clean, minimalist layout that highlights blog posts.

- Integrated commenting and social media sharing options.

- Space for a blog title, tagline, and categories for easy navigation.

To find the perfect blog template, use the search filter to browse through **blog** templates. Wix offers options for both personal blogs and professional blogs, such as those for writers, journalists, or lifestyle influencers.

E-commerce Websites

Building an online store has never been easier with Wix. E-commerce templates are designed to help you create a seamless shopping experience for your customers. Wix's e-commerce templates typically include:

- Product galleries with easy-to-navigate categories.

- A shopping cart system and secure checkout process.

- Integration with payment gateways like PayPal, Stripe, and Wix Payments.

When filtering for **e-commerce** templates, Wix allows you to select a variety of store types, such as **fashion**, **beauty**, **electronics**, or **food and beverage**. You can also choose templates that feature specific tools for **product search**, **inventory management**, and **discounts and promotions**.

Event Websites

If you're planning a wedding, party, or corporate event, Wix has templates designed specifically for creating event websites. These templates typically include:

- RSVP forms for guests.

- Event countdowns and schedules.

- Photo galleries and information sections for event details.

To find event templates, use the **event** filter in the template gallery. Wix offers designs for all kinds of events, from **weddings** and **conferences** to **festivals** and **charity galas**.

Customizing a Template: Basic Customization Options

Once you've selected the perfect template for your website, the next step is customization. Fortunately, Wix's drag-and-drop editor makes it incredibly easy to modify your template without any coding knowledge.

Modifying Text and Fonts

Changing text and fonts is one of the first customizations you'll make. With Wix, you can click directly on any text box to edit the content. Whether you're adding an introductory paragraph or changing a header, the editor lets you update your text instantly.

You can also customize the **fonts** and **text sizes** to match your brand's style. Wix offers a wide selection of web-safe fonts that you can use to customize headings, paragraphs, and buttons. For more advanced typography options, you can upload custom fonts or use Google Fonts integration.

Changing Images and Videos

Replacing images is another straightforward customization. Wix offers a variety of stock images, but you can also upload your media to replace placeholder images. Whether you want to change the hero image on your homepage or update your product images, drag and drop new media into place.

You can also add **background videos** to any section of your site, giving it a dynamic and modern feel. Wix allows you to easily upload and adjust the size of these media files, so you can customize your website exactly how you want it.

Adjusting Colors and Layout

With Wix's easy-to-use editor, you can change the **color scheme** of your website to match your brand. You can modify the colors of your text, buttons, links, and backgrounds with a few clicks. Additionally, Wix gives you the flexibility to adjust the layout of your template, including repositioning sections, resizing elements, and adjusting spacing.

Wix's templates are fully responsive, which means they automatically adjust to look great on any device, but you can also tweak the layout for mobile devices specifically using the **mobile editor**.

Advanced Template Customization: Using Developer Tools (Velo by Wix)

While Wix's drag-and-drop editor provides a simple and intuitive way to customize your website, sometimes you need more control over the design and functionality. This is where **Velo by Wix** comes in. Velo is Wix's developer platform that enables advanced users to add custom functionality and create dynamic, interactive websites.

Introduction to Velo

Velo (formerly known as Corvid) is a powerful tool that allows you to add custom code to your Wix site. With Velo, you can create dynamic pages, integrate third-party APIs, and build custom workflows. Whether you're a developer looking to add a complex feature or an advanced user wanting to expand the functionality of your site, Velo gives you the ability to do so.

Custom Code and APIs

Velo allows you to add **JavaScript code** to your Wix site, giving you complete control over interactions, animations, and data processing. You can also integrate external **APIs** to pull data from other websites or services and display it directly on your site. This is especially useful for creating interactive, data-driven pages such as product catalogs, booking systems, or dynamic galleries.

Creating Dynamic Pages and Databases

One of Velo's standout features is its ability to create dynamic pages. This allows you to build a website where content updates automatically based on a database. For example, you can create a blog that automatically displays new posts from a database or a product catalog that updates as you add new items to your inventory.

You can create and manage your **databases** in Velo, which store your site's data. These databases can be linked to your pages, allowing you to display dynamic content and create custom forms and interactions.

Custom Interactions and Workflows

Velo also lets you create custom interactions and workflows using JavaScript. Whether you want to create an advanced contact form, set up a custom booking system, or design complex animations, Velo gives you the tools to make it happen.

Wix templates offer a fast, convenient way to get started with building a professional website. Whether you're looking for a basic template to get your blog off the ground or a fully-featured template for an online store, Wix has you covered. Customizing a template with Wix's drag-and-drop editor is easy, even for beginners, but the platform also offers advanced customization options for those who want more control over their site. Using Velo by Wix, you can take your customization even further, creating dynamic, data-driven websites with custom code and APIs.

By now, you should feel confident in selecting the right template for your website and understanding how to customize it to fit your needs. In the next chapter, we will explore how to build the structure of your website, add essential pages, and set up a user-friendly navigation system. Whether you're just starting or looking to fine-tune your design, Wix offers all the tools you need to create a beautiful, functional website.

Chapter 3: Designing Your Website with Wix Editor

Designing a website can be an exciting yet overwhelming task, especially if you're not a trained designer or developer. However, with Wix, you have access to a powerful, user-friendly tool that makes the process not only manageable but also enjoyable. The Wix Editor provides a simple drag-and-drop interface that allows you to design and customize every aspect of your website, from the layout and typography to the colors and functionality.

In this chapter, we will guide you through the process of designing your website with the Wix Editor. Whether you're just starting or you're looking to fine-tune your site, we'll cover the essential features of the Wix Editor interface and show you how to effectively add and arrange elements, use grids and containers for better layout control, and customize fonts, colors, and design aesthetics. Additionally, we'll introduce you to Wix's **Artificial Design Intelligence** (Wix ADI), which can automate the design process for those who prefer a hands-off approach. We'll also walk you through the important step of setting up a **mobile-**

responsive design to ensure that your site looks great on all devices.

Introduction to the Wix Editor Interface

The Wix Editor is your creative workspace, providing everything you need to design, customize, and manage your website. When you first enter the Wix Editor, you're presented with a visual interface that's easy to navigate, even for beginners. The Wix Editor is divided into several key sections that allow you to manage different aspects of your site's design and functionality:

- **Main Canvas**: This is the central area where you will design and build your website. It's essentially the "stage" where you drag and drop elements to create your pages. Everything you add, whether it's text, images, or buttons, will be placed and arranged here.

- **Sidebar**: On the left side of the editor, you'll find the sidebar, which houses a variety of tools and options. This is where you can access the elements library, manage site settings, and customize your site's layout and design. Here, you can also access various apps from the Wix

App Market that you can add to your site for additional functionality.

- **Toolbar**: The toolbar at the top of the editor provides quick access to tools like undo/redo, zoom, and preview mode. You'll also find the "Publish" button here, which allows you to publish your site once you're satisfied with your design.

- **Elements Library**: One of the most powerful features of the Wix Editor is the elements library, which can be accessed from the sidebar. Here, you'll find a wide range of elements you can add to your site, including text boxes, images, videos, buttons, social media buttons, forms, and more.

The Wix Editor is designed to be intuitive and flexible, offering all the tools you need to create a fully customized website. Now, let's dive into how to use these tools effectively to build your website.

Adding and Arranging Elements (Text, Images, Videos, Buttons)

The Wix Editor gives you full control over the content and design of your website. The process begins with adding and arranging elements like text, images, videos, and buttons on your page. Here's how you can do this:

Adding Text

To add text to your website, click on the **Text** icon in the elements library and choose from a variety of text options, including **headings**, **subheadings**, **paragraphs**, and **quotes**. Once you've selected a text element, drag it onto your canvas. You can then click directly on the text box to edit the content, adjust the font size, and modify the text formatting.

Wix gives you full control over text customization. You can change the **font family**, **font size**, **color**, **alignment**, and **line spacing**. Additionally, you can use the **text effects** tool to apply shadows, outlines, and animations to your text.

Adding Images and Videos

Images and videos are powerful elements that can make your website more engaging and visually appealing. To add an image, click on the **Image** icon in the elements library, and you'll be given options to either upload your images or select from Wix's vast collection of free stock images.

Once you've added an image, you can resize it, crop it, and reposition it to fit your design. Wix also offers image editing tools that allow you to apply **filters**, **adjust brightness**, and even add **hover effects** for a dynamic user experience.

To add videos, click on the **Video** icon and select either a video from your computer or a video from YouTube, Vimeo, or other external platforms. Wix also offers a **video player** widget that allows you to embed a video on your site, giving you full control over its appearance and functionality.

Adding Buttons

Buttons are essential for creating clear calls to action (CTAs) on your site. Whether it's a "Buy Now" button for an online store, a "Contact Us" button, or a "Learn More" button, Wix allows you to add and customize buttons easily.

To add a button, click on the **Button** icon in the elements library. Once the button is on the canvas, you can change the text, font, color, and size. You can also assign links to the button, directing visitors to specific pages on your site, external links, or a social media profile.

You can also add **hover effects** to buttons to make them interactive. For example, you can change the color of the button or display a subtle animation when users hover over it, providing a more dynamic and engaging user experience.

Working with Grids and Containers for Layout Control

One of the most powerful features of the Wix Editor is its **grid** and **container** system, which helps you organize your website's layout. Grids and containers allow you to align elements neatly and create a cohesive, well-structured design.

Grids

Grids are used to create flexible and responsive website layouts. They allow you to place elements in rows and columns, making it easy to align content consistently across different screen sizes. Wix offers several types of grids, including simple grids for basic layouts and advanced grids for more complex designs.

To add a grid to your page, click on the **Grid** option in the elements library. Once the grid is added to the canvas, you can adjust the number of rows and columns and drag elements into the grid cells. Wix will automatically adjust the elements to fit within the grid's structure, ensuring a clean, organized design.

Containers

Containers are used to group multiple elements and control their alignment and spacing. By using containers, you can move, resize, and align a group of elements as one unit, rather than adjusting each element individually. This is particularly useful when designing responsive layouts that need to adjust to different screen sizes.

To add a container, click on the **Container** option in the elements library, and choose from different container types, such as a **box container** or **strip container**. Once added, you can drag and drop elements into the container and adjust its size, position, and spacing.

Customizing Fonts, Colors, and Design Aesthetics

Customizing your website's fonts and colors is crucial for creating a unique and professional design that reflects your brand or personal style. Wix offers a wide range of design customization options, from fonts and color palettes to background images and design effects.

Fonts and Typography

Typography plays a huge role in your website's overall look and feel. To customize the fonts, click on the **Text** element you want to modify and use the toolbar to adjust the font family, size, and style. Wix offers an extensive collection of fonts, including both classic and modern choices. If you have a specific font in mind, you can even upload custom fonts to use on your site.

To ensure consistency, you can set a default font style for the entire site by clicking on the **Site Design** option in the editor and selecting **Typography**. From here, you can adjust the font settings for headings, subheadings, paragraphs, and buttons.

Colors and Palettes

Choosing the right color scheme for your website is essential for creating a visually appealing design. Wix provides a variety of **color palettes** to help you select complementary colors for your site. You can either choose one of the pre-designed color schemes or create your custom palette by selecting colors for elements like **text**, **backgrounds**, and **buttons**.

To customize colors, click on any element (e.g., a text box or button) and use the toolbar to change the color. Wix also allows you to adjust transparency and gradients, enabling you to create subtle color effects that enhance the visual appeal of your site.

Backgrounds and Effects

Wix allows you to customize the background of your website or individual sections. You can choose from a **solid color**, **gradient**, **image**, or **video** background. Background images can be uploaded from your collection or selected from Wix's library of stock images.

To create dynamic effects, you can add **parallax scrolling** to your background images, which creates a smooth scrolling effect when users move down the page. This effect can add a sense of depth and movement to your site, making it more engaging and interactive.

Using Wix ADI (Artificial Design Intelligence) for Automated Design

For those who prefer a more automated approach to website design, Wix offers **Wix ADI (Artificial Design Intelligence)**. Wix ADI is a tool that uses artificial intelligence to automatically create a personalized website for you based on your preferences and inputs. It's perfect for users who want to get a website up and running quickly without spending time on design details.

To use Wix ADI, click on the **Wix ADI** option when creating a new site. You'll be asked a series of questions about your site's purpose, industry, and style preferences. Wix ADI will then generate a custom design based on your answers. You can further customize the design using the Wix Editor, making it easy to tweak the site until it perfectly matches your vision.

Wix ADI is a great choice for those who need a professional-looking website but don't have the time or expertise to design it from scratch. While it's more automated than using the Wix Editor directly, it still provides plenty of customization options to ensure that your site reflects your brand.

Setting Up Mobile-Responsive Design for Your Site

In today's world, it's essential to ensure that your website looks great on all devices, including smartphones and tablets. Wix's Editor is built with mobile responsiveness in mind, meaning that your site will automatically adjust its layout for different screen sizes. However, you can also fine-tune the mobile version of your website to make sure it delivers an optimal user experience.

To edit the mobile version of your site, click on the **Mobile** icon in the top toolbar of the Wix Editor. This will open a mobile-specific version of your site, where you can make adjustments such as:

- **Repositioning elements**: You can move, resize, or hide elements specifically for mobile users to ensure the layout is optimized for smaller screens.

- **Changing font sizes**: Text might appear too small on mobile devices, so you can adjust the font size to improve readability.

- **Editing buttons and links**: Ensure that buttons and links are large enough to tap easily on mobile devices.

Once you're happy with the mobile version, save your changes and preview the mobile site to ensure it works seamlessly across different devices.

Designing your website with the Wix Editor is straightforward and rewarding. It allows you to create a unique, professional-looking website without the need for coding knowledge. By understanding the tools available in the Wix Editor, including the ability to add and arrange elements, use grids and containers, and customize fonts, colors, and layout, you can design a site that perfectly reflects your vision. Additionally, Wix's **Artificial Design Intelligence (Wix ADI)** provides a quick, automated solution for those who prefer a hands-off approach.

Lastly, Wix makes it easy to ensure that your site is mobile-responsive, allowing it to look great on any device. Whether you're a beginner or an experienced web designer, Wix offers the flexibility and power you need to create a stunning website. In the next chapter, we'll explore how to build your website's structure and ensure your navigation is user-friendly, making it easy for visitors to find the information they need.

Wix Website

Chapter 4: Building Your Website's Structure

Designing a visually appealing website is only one part of the process. To truly make your site functional, user-friendly, and easy to navigate, it's crucial to build a strong and organized structure. The structure of your website determines how users interact with it, how content is displayed, and how easy it is for visitors to find the information they're looking for. Whether you're running a personal blog, a business site, or an e-commerce store, a well-organized structure enhances user experience (UX), increases engagement, and can contribute to higher conversion rates.

In this chapter, we will cover the essentials of building your website's structure on Wix. From creating and organizing pages and subpages to designing a logical navigation menu, this chapter will help you set up a website that not only looks great but also works seamlessly. Additionally, we will provide tips for creating essential pages like your homepage, about page, contact page, and more. Whether you're just starting or are looking to refine your existing structure, this chapter will provide the knowledge and guidance you need to take your site to the next level.

Creating Pages and Subpages

The foundation of your website's structure begins with its pages. Pages are the primary building blocks of your website, each serving a specific purpose and presenting a specific type of content. Depending on the nature of your website, these pages might include a homepage, product or service pages, an about page, a blog, a contact page, and many others.

When creating pages for your website, it's important to think about the flow of information. You want visitors to easily find what they're looking for without having to click through too many pages. Let's break down the process of creating pages and subpages on Wix:

Creating a Page

To create a page in the Wix Editor, follow these steps:

1. **Go to the Editor**: Log in to your Wix account and open your website in the Wix Editor.

2. **Click on "Menus & Pages"**: In the left-hand sidebar, click on "Menus & Pages" to access your site's page management options.

3. **Add a New Page**: At the bottom of the page list, click on the **"+ Add Page"** button. You'll be

prompted to choose a type of page (e.g., standard page, blog, or product page), or you can create a blank page.

4. **Name the Page**: After adding the page, give it a relevant name (e.g., "Home," "About Us," or "Products"). The page name will appear in your navigation menu, so it's important to choose a name that clearly communicates the page's content.

Once you've created a page, you can start adding elements such as text, images, videos, buttons, and forms. The Wix Editor allows you to design the layout and content of each page, making it easy to customize your website's structure.

Creating Subpages

Subpages are pages that fall under a primary parent page in the website hierarchy. For example, if you have a main page called "Services," you might create subpages for each specific service, such as "Web Design," "Consulting," or "Marketing." Subpages allow you to organize your content and break it down into more manageable sections, improving the user experience.

To create a subpage in Wix, follow these steps:

1. **Go to "Menus & Pages"**: In the Wix Editor, click on "Menus & Pages" again to view your site's page list.

2. **Select a Parent Page**: Click on the page that will serve as the parent page (e.g., "Services").

3. **Add Subpage**: Click on the "+" icon next to the parent page to create a subpage. Give the subpage a relevant name and start designing it.

Subpages will automatically appear in your navigation menu, typically under their respective parent pages. You can control the order in which pages appear in the menu and determine whether a subpage is visible in the main navigation or nested under the parent page.

Organizing Your Website Navigation Menu

Your website's navigation menu is the primary way visitors will interact with your site. A clear, well-organized menu makes it easy for users to find the content they need, which can significantly improve their experience and engagement. A confusing or cluttered navigation menu can frustrate users, leading them to leave your site before they've had a chance to explore it fully.

When setting up your website's navigation menu, there are a few important considerations to keep in mind:

Simplifying the Menu

One of the most important principles of website navigation is simplicity. Avoid overwhelming visitors with too many options in the main navigation menu. Instead, focus on the most important pages and categories. Aim for a clean, minimal menu with no more than five to seven primary menu items. These could include pages like:

- **IIome**

- **About Us**

- **Services/Products**

- **Blog**

- **Contact**

If you have additional pages, consider organizing them under dropdown menus or in the footer so they're accessible but don't clutter the main navigation.

Organizing with Dropdown Menus

For larger websites with multiple sections, dropdown menus are a great way to keep the navigation organized without overwhelming users. Wix makes it easy to create dropdown menus by nesting subpages under their parent pages. For example, if you have a "Services" page, you can create a dropdown menu that includes links to each of your services, like "Web Design," "SEO," and "Consulting."

To create a dropdown menu in Wix:

1. **Go to "Menus & Pages"**: In the Wix Editor, click on "Menus & Pages."

2. **Add a Subpage**: Create subpages for each of the categories you want to include in the dropdown menu.

3. **Arrange Pages**: Drag and drop subpages under their parent pages in the page list.

4. **Customize the Menu**: Wix will automatically generate the dropdown menu, but you can customize its appearance and behavior to fit your site's design.

Dropdown menus are essential for organizing large amounts of content, allowing visitors to find what they're looking for quickly.

Fixed or Sticky Navigation

A **sticky navigation bar** stays visible at the top of the screen as users scroll down the page. This is especially useful for longer pages or websites with lots of content. Wix allows you to easily create a fixed navigation bar that will follow users as they navigate your site.

To enable sticky navigation in Wix:

1. **Go to "Menus & Pages"**: Click on "Menus & Pages" in the Wix Editor.

2. **Select Navigation Bar**: Select the navigation bar and click on the settings icon.

3. **Enable Sticky Feature**: In the settings, toggle on the "Sticky" option to make the navigation bar remain visible as visitors scroll.

Sticky navigation helps users access your menu at any point without having to scroll back to the top of the page.

Best Practices for a User-Friendly Website Structure

Building an organized, user-friendly website structure is about more than just creating pages. It's also about ensuring that visitors can find information quickly and easily. Here are some best practices for building a website structure that is intuitive, easy to navigate, and accessible:

Keep the User Journey in Mind

When designing your website structure, always consider the user journey. Think about how users will move from one page to another and interact with your content. Ensure that your navigation menu leads users logically from one section of your site to the next. For example, visitors to an e-commerce site should be able to find products quickly, view them in detail, add them to the cart, and easily check out.

Consider organizing content in a way that minimizes the number of clicks users need to find what they're looking for. Don't bury important information on subpages that are hard to find.

Use Clear and Descriptive Page Titles

Your page titles should be clear, concise, and descriptive. The title is what users will see in the navigation menu, so it should accurately reflect the page's content. For example, instead of naming a page "Products," name it something more specific, like "Our Web Design Services" or "Custom Furniture Shop."

Avoid using jargon or vague terms that might confuse visitors. Be as descriptive as possible without overloading the title with too many words.

Implement Internal Linking

Internal linking is the practice of linking to other pages within your website. This helps visitors discover more content and improves the overall usability of your site. When creating your pages, consider adding links to related content within the body of the page. For example, on your blog posts, you can link to other related articles or services that might interest the reader.

Internal linking also helps with SEO (search engine optimization), as it helps search engines understand the structure of your site and crawl it more efficiently.

Provide a Search Function

For larger websites with lots of content, it's important to include a **search bar** that allows visitors to find specific information quickly. Wix allows you to easily add a search bar to your site, either as a fixed element in the header or as a dedicated page.

To add a search bar in Wix:

1. **Go to the Wix Editor**: In the left-hand toolbar, click on the **Add** icon.

2. **Select "Search"**: Choose from different search bar options and drag it to your site's header or sidebar.

A search function enhances the user experience, making it easy for visitors to find specific content without having to navigate through multiple pages.

Setting Up a Homepage, About Page, Contact Page, and More

Once you've created your website's overall structure, it's time to focus on the essential pages. These pages serve as the backbone of your site, providing visitors with crucial information about your brand, products, or services. Here's how to set up some of the most important pages on your website:

Homepage

Your homepage is the first impression visitors will have of your site, so it's crucial to make it visually appealing and user-friendly. It should clearly convey what your website is about and guide visitors to other parts of your site. Consider including the following elements:

- **Hero Section**: A large, attention-grabbing image or video with a clear call to action.

- **Introduction**: A brief introduction to your business or personal brand.

- **Navigation**: Easy access to key pages such as your products, services, or blog.

- **Testimonials/Reviews**: Positive feedback from customers or clients.

- **Footer**: Links to your privacy policy, social media, and contact information.

About Page

Your **About Page** provides visitors with important background information about your brand, mission, and values. It should convey trust and authenticity. Include the following elements:

- **Company Overview**: A brief description of your business or personal brand.

- **Mission Statement**: What drives your business or personal brand?

- **Team Information**: Introduce your team or collaborators with photos and bios.

- **Values**: Communicate your core values and what makes you stand out from competitors.

Contact Page

The **Contact Page** is one of the most important pages on your site. It provides visitors with a way to get in touch with you, whether for inquiries, support, or feedback. Include the following elements:

- **Contact Form**: A simple form for visitors to send inquiries or messages.

- **Email Address**: An email address for direct communication.

- **Phone Number**: If applicable, provide a contact number for immediate assistance.

- **Social Media Links**: Links to your social media profiles for additional contact options.

By following these best practices, you can create a website structure that is organized, user-friendly, and optimized for both visitors and search engines.

Building a website's structure is more than just creating pages; it's about designing an intuitive, user-friendly experience that allows visitors to find the information they need quickly and easily. By organizing your pages and subpages, setting up a clear and simple navigation menu, and following best practices for layout and internal linking, you can create a site that's both functional and visually appealing. Additionally, by focusing on essential pages like your homepage, about page, and contact page, you ensure that your website has the core components needed to engage and inform visitors. In the next chapter, we will dive into essential elements like SEO optimization and how to ensure your site is visible and easy to find.

Chapter 5: Essential Wix Features for Beginners

Building a website with Wix is not just about creating a visually appealing design. To make your site interactive, engaging, and functional, it's important to integrate features that enhance user experience, streamline interactions, and expand your site's capabilities. Wix provides a wide range of built-in features and tools that are easy to use, even for beginners. These features can help you improve engagement, boost traffic, and offer additional services to your visitors.

In this chapter, we will cover some of the most essential Wix features that beginners should be aware of. From adding and customizing forms for user interaction to incorporating social media feeds, integrating external tools like Google Maps, and setting up a blog or online store, this chapter will provide you with a solid understanding of the powerful features available to you. We will also look at how to utilize the **Wix App Market** to extend the functionality of your website further. Whether you're building a personal blog, a business site, or an online store, these features will help you take your website to the next level.

Adding and Customizing Forms for User Interaction

Forms are one of the most essential tools on any website. They allow users to interact with your site, whether by signing up for a newsletter, making inquiries, or submitting feedback. Forms can help you collect valuable information from your visitors and provide a way for them to connect with you directly. Wix makes it easy to add and customize forms, even if you have no prior experience with web development.

Adding a Form

To add a form to your Wix website:

1. **Go to the Wix Editor**: Open your site in the Wix Editor.

2. **Select the "Add" Button**: In the left sidebar, click on the "Add" button (represented by a plus icon).

3. **Choose "Forms"**: From the dropdown menu, select "Forms." Wix provides a variety of form options, including contact forms, subscription forms, event registration forms, and custom forms.

4. **Drag and Drop the Form**: Once you've chosen a form type, drag it to the location where you want it to appear on your page.

5. **Customize the Form**: After placing the form, you can click on it to customize it. Wix allows you to add or remove fields, change labels, and adjust settings such as the field type (e.g., text, email, dropdown, etc.).

Wix's form editor is straightforward and intuitive. Depending on your needs, you can create simple contact forms or more complex forms with multiple fields.

Customizing the Form

Wix offers several ways to customize the form to suit your site's design and functionality. Some customization options include:

- **Changing Form Fields**: Wix allows you to add custom fields based on the type of information you want to collect. For instance, you can add fields for name, email, message, phone number, and more. You can also make fields required to ensure users provide the necessary information.

- **Styling the Form**: Customize the look of your form by adjusting the colors, fonts, and button styles. You can also change the form layout to match your website's design.

- **Setting Up Form Submissions**: Once the form is complete, you can set up how the form submissions are handled. Wix allows you to receive form submissions via email or store them in your Wix account for easy management.

Forms are an essential feature for any website because they provide a direct channel for communication with your visitors. Whether you're collecting leads, handling customer inquiries, or simply gathering feedback, forms are a powerful tool for engaging your audience.

Incorporating Social Media Feeds and Sharing Options

Social media has become an essential part of online engagement. It allows you to connect with your audience, share content, and drive traffic back to your website. Integrating social media feeds and sharing options into your Wix website can help increase your site's visibility and make it more interactive. Wix offers several tools to make social media integration quick and easy.

Adding Social Media Buttons

To add social media buttons to your website:

1. **Go to the Wix Editor**: Open your site in the Wix Editor.

2. **Select the "Add" Button**: Click on the "Add" button on the left sidebar.

3. **Choose "Social"**: Under the "Social" section, you'll find options for adding social media buttons (e.g., Facebook, Twitter, Instagram, LinkedIn, Pinterest, and others).

4. **Drag and Drop the Buttons**: Drag the social media icons to the area of the page where you want them to appear. Typically, social media buttons are placed in a website's header or footer, but you can place them anywhere on your page.

5. **Link Your Social Media Accounts**: Once you've placed the buttons, you can link each button to your social media profiles by clicking

on the icon and entering the appropriate URL for each social network.

Adding Social Media Feeds

Displaying social media feeds on your website is an excellent way to showcase your social presence and keep your site fresh with up-to-date content. Wix makes it easy to add live social media feeds to your site. For example, you can display your Instagram feed, Twitter feed, or Facebook posts.

To add a social media feed:

1. **Go to the Wix App Market**: In the Wix Editor, click on the **App Market** button in the left sidebar.

2. **Search for the Social Media Feed**: Type in the name of the platform you want to integrate (e.g., "Instagram Feed" or "Facebook Feed").

3. **Select an App**: Choose the app you want to add to your site. Some apps are free, while others may require a paid plan.

4. **Install the App**: Click the "Add to Site" button, and follow the prompts to connect your social media account to the app.

5. **Customize the Feed**: Once the feed is installed, you can customize its appearance. You can adjust the size, layout, and style to match your site's design.

Social media feeds are a great way to display dynamic content on your website, keep visitors engaged, and encourage them to follow you on social media.

Integrating Google Maps and Other External Tools

Google Maps is a powerful tool that allows you to embed a map of your location on your website. This is especially useful for businesses with physical storefronts or service areas. By adding a map to your site, you make it easier for customers to find your location and navigate to your business. Wix allows you to easily integrate Google Maps and other external tools, enhancing the functionality of your website.

Adding Google Maps

To add Google Maps to your Wix site:

1. **Go to the Wix Editor**: Open your website in the Wix Editor.

2. **Select the "Add" Button**: Click the "Add" button on the left sidebar.

3. **Choose "More" and Select "Google Maps"**: Under the "More" section, click on "Google Maps." This will allow you to add a map to your site.

4. **Enter Your Location**: After placing the map on your page, enter your business address or location in the settings. Wix will automatically display the map with the correct location.

5. **Customize the Map**: You can adjust the map's size, zoom level, and design to fit your website's style. You can also add markers and labels and customize the colors.

Integrating Google Maps is a simple but effective way to improve your website's functionality and make it easier for users to find your physical location.

Integrating Other External Tools

Wix also allows you to integrate a wide range of external tools and services to enhance your site's functionality. For example, you can add tools for live chat, booking systems, email marketing, analytics, and more. To do this, you can browse the **Wix App Market**, which offers a wide selection of third-party apps that integrate seamlessly with your Wix site.

Some popular external tools include:

- **Live Chat**: Tools like **Tidio** or **Wix Chat** allow you to add live chat functionality to your site, making it easier for visitors to ask questions or get support.

- **Booking Systems**: If you run a service-based business, you can integrate booking tools like **Wix Bookings** to allow customers to schedule appointments online.

- **Email Marketing**: Integrate email marketing tools like **Mailchimp** or **Wix ShoutOut** to create and send newsletters to your subscribers.

By integrating these external tools, you can create a more personalized and functional website that meets the needs of your business and customers.

Setting Up a Blog Section

A blog is a great way to engage with your audience, share valuable content, and improve your website's SEO. With Wix, setting up a blog is incredibly easy.

Whether you're a hobbyist blogger or a business looking to share industry insights, Wix provides all the tools you need to create and manage a blog on your website.

Adding a Blog Section

To add a blog to your Wix site:

1. **Go to the Wix Editor**: Open your website in the Wix Editor.

2. **Select the "Add" Button**: Click on the "Add" button in the left sidebar.

3. **Choose "Blog"**: Select the "Blog" option under the "Add" section.

4. **Choose Your Blog Layout**: Wix offers several pre-designed blog layouts that you can choose from. Pick one that matches your site's design and click "Add to Site."

5. **Customize Your Blog**: Once the blog is added, you can customize the layout, design, and content of your blog. Wix allows you to adjust font styles, colors, and the arrangement of blog posts. You can also create categories to

organize your posts and add tags to make it easier for visitors to find specific content.

Wix's blog tool makes it simple to create a professional-looking blog that integrates seamlessly with your site's design. You can post articles, add images and videos, and allow visitors to leave comments.

Adding an Online Store: Introduction to Wix eCommerce

Wix makes it easy to create a fully functional online store. Whether you're selling physical products, digital downloads, or services, Wix provides all the tools you need to set up a secure and user-friendly e-commerce store.

Setting Up an Online Store

To set up an online store on Wix:

1. **Go to the Wix Editor**: Open your website in the Wix Editor.

2. **Select the "Add" Button**: Click on the "Add" button and choose the **Store** option.

3. **Add Products**: You'll be prompted to set up your store and add products. You can upload images, set prices, and provide product descriptions.

4. **Set Up Payment Options**: Wix allows you to choose from a variety of payment gateways, including **Wix Payments**, **PayPal**, and **Stripe**.

5. **Customize Your Store**: You can customize the layout of your online store, choose different themes, and add features like product categories, filters, and reviews.

Wix's eCommerce tools make it easy to set up a professional online store, complete with shopping carts, secure payment processing, and inventory management.

Utilizing the Wix App Market for Added Functionality

The **Wix App Market** is a valuable resource for adding extra functionality to your site. Whether you need SEO tools, social media integrations, marketing apps, or advanced analytics, the Wix App Market offers a variety of third-party apps that can integrate seamlessly with your site.

To browse the Wix App Market:

1. **Go to the Wix Editor**: In the left sidebar of the Wix Editor, click on the **App Market** button.

2. **Browse and Install Apps**: You can browse apps by category or use the search bar to find specific apps. Click on an app to read more about it, and click "Add to Site" to install it.

Some popular Wix apps include:

- **SEO Tools**: Apps like **Wix SEO Wiz** can help you optimize your website for search engines.

- **Email Marketing**: Apps like **Mailchimp** and **Wix ShoutOut** allow you to easily create and send marketing emails.

- **Live Chat**: Apps like **Tidio** or **Wix Chat** add live chat features to your site, allowing you to engage with visitors in real-time.

The Wix App Market offers endless possibilities for expanding the functionality of your website, helping you meet your goals and deliver a better experience for your users.

Wix offers an array of powerful features that are easy to use, even for beginners. From adding and customizing forms to incorporating social media feeds, setting up blogs, and building an online store, Wix provides all the tools you need to create an interactive, engaging, and functional website. By integrating external tools like Google Maps, utilizing the Wix App Market, and enhancing your site's e-commerce capabilities, you can build a website that meets your specific needs and delivers a top-notch user experience. These essential features will help you take your website to the next level, whether you're creating a personal blog, a business site, or an online store.

Chapter 6: Advanced Wix Features for Pros

Wix has revolutionized the website-building process by providing an intuitive, user-friendly platform that allows anyone—from beginners to experienced designers—to create stunning websites. However, for those with more advanced needs or technical expertise, Wix offers a range of powerful tools and features that can be fully customized to suit a variety of business models and creative projects. This chapter will guide you through some of the more advanced features Wix has to offer, including **Wix Velo** (formerly known as Corvid), custom backend functionality, building dynamic databases, integrating third-party tools, and creating custom Wix applications.

Whether you are an experienced web developer looking to add custom code to your site, an entrepreneur who needs a tailored business solution, or a designer who wants to build a completely unique user experience, Wix has the tools and flexibility you need. Let's explore these advanced features and how they can help you take your website to the next level.

Using Wix Velo (Formerly Corvid) for Full-Code Control

For developers or experienced users who need more control over the functionality of their site, **Wix Velo** (formerly known as **Corvid by Wix**) is an invaluable tool. Velo is Wix's open development platform that allows you to write and integrate custom JavaScript code into your website, offering full control over the behavior and interactivity of your site. This feature opens up a world of possibilities, from adding complex animations and interactions to creating dynamic, data-driven websites.

What is Wix Velo?

Wix Velo is a development platform built into the Wix Editor, designed to allow users to add custom functionality, create complex applications, and manage backend services—all without leaving the Wix environment. Velo is built on standard web technologies such as **JavaScript**, **APIs**, and **Databases**, making it accessible for anyone with coding knowledge to extend their Wix website's functionality.

By enabling Velo, users gain access to:

- **Custom Code**: Write your own JavaScript code and integrate it seamlessly with your site.

- **APIs**: Use REST APIs to send and receive data from other services, allowing for deeper integration and real-time updates.

- **Databases**: Create and manage databases to store content, user data, and other site-related information.

Getting Started with Wix Velo

To start using Velo, follow these simple steps:

1. **Open the Wix Editor**: Log in to your Wix account and open your site in the Wix Editor.

2. **Enable Velo**: In the top menu, click on the "Dev Mode" option and toggle the **Velo** option on. This will reveal the code editor and backend features that come with Velo.

3. **Write Custom Code**: Once Velo is enabled, you can begin writing JavaScript code that will be applied to different parts of your site. The code editor allows you to write, test, and debug JavaScript code directly within the Wix platform.

4. **Create Backend Functions**: You can create backend functions using JavaScript that interact with the front-end elements of your site. For example, you can create forms, validation rules, and custom user flows that operate in real-time.

With Wix Velo, you can access server-side APIs, create dynamic data sets, and build custom workflows without ever needing to leave the Wix platform. Whether you need to build a booking system, create a custom member portal, or integrate payment processing, Wix Velo makes it easy to take your website to the next level.

Customizing Backend Functionality with JavaScript and APIs

For advanced users and developers, Wix Velo offers the ability to add custom **backend functionality** to your site using JavaScript. This allows you to create highly interactive, dynamic sites with rich user experiences.

JavaScript and Wix Velo

JavaScript is one of the core languages of web development, and Wix Velo lets you seamlessly integrate it into your Wix site. Whether you're building custom forms, creating dynamic elements, or working with APIs, JavaScript gives you the ability to implement complex functionality.

Here are a few examples of what you can do with JavaScript in Wix Velo:

- **Form Validation**: Create custom validation rules for user input, such as checking if a phone number is valid or if the email entered is in the correct format.

- **Conditional Logic**: Write JavaScript code to implement conditional logic on your website. For example, you can show or hide certain elements based on user actions (such as selecting a particular option in a dropdown menu).

- **Interactivity**: Enhance user engagement by adding interactive features such as image sliders, lightboxes, or pop-up windows that appear when certain conditions are met.

Using APIs with Wix Velo

Wix Velo allows you to integrate **third-party APIs** into your site, making it possible to connect with external tools, services, and data sources. Using REST APIs, you can send and receive data between your Wix site and other services. This is useful for integrating features such as:

- **Payment Gateways**: Integrate payment APIs like PayPal or Stripe to accept online payments.

- **External Databases**: Connect to external databases to pull in or store data on your site, such as user profiles or product information.

- **External Services**: Connect your website to tools such as marketing platforms, email services, or even social media accounts to streamline workflows and enhance functionality.

To integrate an API, you would typically use the fetch() function in JavaScript within Wix Velo to send and receive data. The ability to interact with external services opens up endless possibilities for adding dynamic content and creating highly customized user experiences.

Building a Custom Database for Dynamic Content Management

For many websites, dynamic content—content that changes based on user input, behavior, or data—is essential. With Wix Velo, you can build a **custom database** to manage this dynamic content.

What is a Custom Database in Wix Velo?

Wix Velo allows you to create custom databases that store content, such as product listings, blog posts, user-generated content, or any other type of data that needs to be displayed on your website. These databases can be fully integrated with your website, making it easy to update content dynamically and present information to users in real-time.

Creating a Database in Wix Velo

To create a custom database:

1. **Enable Velo**: First, make sure you have enabled Velo in the Wix Editor.

2. **Add a Database**: In the Velo sidebar, click on the **Database** icon and choose "Create New

Collection." This will allow you to define the structure of your database, including the fields (e.g., text, number, date) and data types you want to store.

3. **Define Data Fields**: For example, if you're creating a product database, you might define fields such as **product name**, **price**, **description**, and **image**. You can also define which fields are required and which can be left empty.

4. **Connect Your Database to the Frontend**: Once the database is set up, you can bind it to various elements on your website. For example, you can display a list of products dynamically by connecting your product database to a **Repeater** or **Dynamic Page** element in the Wix Editor. This allows the content to update automatically whenever the data in the database changes.

Managing Dynamic Content

With Wix Velo, you can create **Dynamic Pages** that automatically populate with content from your database. Dynamic Pages allow you to display content that is unique to each user or item. For example, an e-commerce website can display a unique product page for each item, pulling content such as images, descriptions, and pricing from the product database.

Additionally, Wix allows you to create **content filtering** for dynamic pages. For instance, you can filter and display blog posts, products, or events based on categories, tags, or other criteria.

Integrating Third-Party Tools and Services with Wix

While Wix provides a wide range of built-in tools and features, there are times when you might want to integrate third-party tools and services into your website. Wix Velo makes this process easy by allowing you to connect your site to external APIs, services, and tools to enhance functionality.

Popular Third-Party Integrations

1. **Payment Systems**: If you're running an online store or accepting donations, integrating payment systems such as **PayPal**, **Stripe**, or **Square** is essential. Wix provides out-of-the-box integration for some payment processors,

but if you need more flexibility, you can use custom APIs to connect to additional services.

2. **Marketing Tools**: For marketing automation, integrating third-party tools like **Mailchimp**, **HubSpot**, or **Zapier** can streamline your processes. For example, you can set up workflows to automatically send out newsletters when new blog posts are published.

3. **Social Media**: Connect your website to social media platforms like **Instagram**, **Facebook**, or **Twitter** to display feeds, run ads, or facilitate sharing. You can integrate these services into your site using their official APIs or third-party apps available in the **Wix App Market**.

Setting Up Third-Party Integrations

To integrate third-party tools:

1. **Go to the Wix Editor**: Open your website in the Wix Editor.

2. **Add a New API**: In Velo, click on the **Code** icon in the sidebar and select **External API** to set up a connection with an external service.

3. **Follow API Documentation**: Each API comes with its own documentation on how to integrate it with your site. Follow the instructions carefully to ensure a smooth integration.

Using third-party tools allows you to extend your website's capabilities, making it more powerful and aligned with your business or creative needs.

Creating and Managing Custom Wix Applications

In addition to creating custom functionality and integrating external services, Wix Velo allows you to build **custom applications** tailored to your specific requirements. Whether you need a custom dashboard, a booking system, or a unique form, Wix enables you to create bespoke applications using JavaScript and APIs.

What is a Custom Wix Application?

A **custom Wix application** is a fully functional, standalone app built within the Wix ecosystem. These apps can include custom pages, logic, and interactions that are specific to your website. With Velo, you can build and deploy apps that offer specialized functionality, such as customer portals, booking systems, or event management tools.

Steps to Create a Custom Wix Application

1. **Enable Velo**: Make sure Velo is enabled on your Wix site.

2. **Write Custom Code**: Use JavaScript to create your app's logic and functionality. You can also access Wix's built-in libraries and APIs to interact with your site's data.

3. **Create a User Interface**: Design the app's user interface (UI) using the Wix Editor. You can add buttons, text fields, and other elements to create a user-friendly experience.

4. **Test the App**: Before going live, use Velo's testing environment to debug and optimize your app.

5. **Deploy Your Application**: Once your app is complete, you can deploy it directly to your site or even make it available for other Wix users in the **Wix App Market**.

Wix offers a robust set of advanced features that allow experienced users to take their websites beyond the basics. With **Wix Velo**, you can implement custom code, manage dynamic content, and integrate third-party tools to create fully functional, highly interactive websites. Whether you're building a complex e-commerce platform, creating custom applications, or managing a database-driven site, Wix provides the flexibility and power you need to bring your vision to life. These advanced features give you the tools to create a truly unique online experience for your visitors, and they're accessible directly within the Wix platform.

Chapter 7: SEO and Site Optimization

Creating a beautiful and functional website is only part of the equation when it comes to achieving success in the online world. The other critical aspect is making sure that your website is **discoverable** by your target audience. No matter how impressive your website looks or how well it functions, if it doesn't appear on search engines like Google, you'll be missing out on valuable traffic and potential customers. This is where **Search Engine Optimization** (SEO) comes into play.

In this chapter, we will dive deep into the world of **SEO** and **site optimization** for Wix websites. We'll explore how to use **Wix's SEO Wiz** tool, which is designed to simplify the process of optimizing your website for search engines, and walk through best practices for on-page SEO. We'll also discuss crucial factors like **site speed**, **performance optimization**, and **Google Analytics integration**, along with strategies for **mobile optimization**—all of which are essential to ensure that your site performs well and ranks high on search engines.

Whether you're a beginner just starting to learn about SEO or an experienced website owner looking to refine your approach, this chapter will provide valuable insights and actionable steps to help you succeed in the digital landscape.

Introduction to Wix's SEO Wiz Tool and Its Importance

Wix offers a powerful tool called **SEO Wiz**, which is designed to make search engine optimization easier for everyone, even those who don't have technical knowledge of SEO. SEO Wiz is a step-by-step guide that takes you through the process of optimizing your Wix website for search engines, offering personalized recommendations based on your industry, keywords, and goals. This tool simplifies the process of improving your website's visibility in search engine results, making it much more accessible for beginners.

What is Wix's SEO Wiz Tool?

The SEO Wiz tool in Wix helps you optimize your website by offering suggestions and actionable steps for improving its SEO. When you first enable the SEO Wiz, you'll be asked to input information about your site, such as:

- **Your website's name and industry**

- **Target keywords and phrases**

- **Your site's main goal (e.g., lead generation, sales, etc.)**

Based on this information, Wix will generate a personalized SEO plan for your website. The plan typically includes tasks such as:

- **Optimizing page titles and meta descriptions**

- **Choosing and using the right keywords**

- **Improving image alt text**

- **Ensuring your website is mobile-friendly**

One of the biggest advantages of SEO Wiz is that it provides specific, actionable tasks to improve your SEO performance. Instead of requiring a deep understanding of SEO techniques, SEO Wiz guides you through the necessary steps to boost your website's search engine ranking.

The Importance of SEO for Your Wix Website

SEO is essential for your website's success because it directly impacts your ability to rank on search engines like Google, Bing, and Yahoo. Without SEO, your site may remain buried in search engine results, making it difficult for potential visitors to find you. A well-optimized website can:

- **Increase Visibility**: With proper SEO, your website will rank higher in search engine results, leading to more organic traffic.

- **Attract Targeted Traffic**: SEO ensures that your website is visible to people who are actively searching for the products, services, or content you offer.

- **Build Credibility**: Higher search rankings can build trust and credibility with your audience, as people often associate high-ranking sites with authority and reliability.

- **Improve User Experience**: Optimizing your website for SEO often includes improving site speed, content organization, and navigation—all of which contribute to a better user experience.

Incorporating SEO best practices into your Wix site will help you stay competitive, attract more visitors, and achieve your business or personal goals.

Best Practices for On-Page SEO (Meta Tags, Alt Texts, Keywords)

On-page SEO refers to all the actions you take directly on your website to improve its search engine ranking. This includes optimizing elements like **meta tags**, **image alt text**, **keywords**, and **content structure**. Let's explore some of the most important aspects of on-page SEO and how to optimize them for better search engine performance.

Meta Tags: Titles and Descriptions

Meta tags provide important information about your web pages to search engines and visitors. Two of the most important meta tags are **title tags** and **meta descriptions**. These tags are displayed in search engine results, so they play a significant role in influencing click-through rates (CTR).

- **Title Tags**: The title tag is one of the most important on-page SEO elements. It tells both search engines and users what the page is about. The title should be concise (under 60 characters), include relevant keywords, and be unique for each page.

For example, a good title for a blog post about "How to Build a Wix Website" might be: *"How to Build a Wix Website: Step-by-Step Guide for Beginners"*

- **Meta Descriptions**: The meta description appears below the title in search engine results. It provides a brief summary of what the page is about and can influence users to click on the link. Meta descriptions should be under 160 characters, contain relevant keywords, and provide a compelling reason for users to visit the page.

Example:
"Learn how to build a Wix website from scratch with this easy-to-follow, step-by-step guide. Perfect for beginners!"

Wix allows you to customize both your title tags and meta descriptions for each page through the **SEO settings**. Make sure to create unique and keyword-rich titles and descriptions for all important pages on your website.

Image Alt Text

Image optimization is an important aspect of SEO that many website owners overlook. Since search engines can't "see" images, they rely on **alt text** (alternative text) to understand what the image represents. Alt text not only helps with SEO but also improves **accessibility** for users with disabilities.

To optimize your images:

1. **Add Descriptive Alt Text**: When adding an image to your Wix site, ensure that each image has a descriptive alt text that includes relevant keywords. The alt text should describe the image and be concise.

Example:
For an image of a website design, use an alt text like:
"Web design inspiration on a Wix website homepage"

2. **Use Keywords Naturally**: Incorporating keywords into your image alt text helps improve your site's relevance for those keywords.

Keywords: Research and Placement

Keywords are the foundation of SEO. They are the terms and phrases people search for when looking for content or products like yours. Conducting thorough keyword research and strategically placing those keywords throughout your website's content is critical for improving your rankings.

- **Keyword Research**: Use tools like Google Keyword Planner, SEMrush, or Ubersuggest to find relevant keywords for your website. Focus on both **short-tail** keywords (e.g., "website design") and **long-tail** keywords (e.g., "how to design a website with Wix").

- **Placing Keywords**: Once you have a list of keywords, place them strategically on your site. This includes using them in your title tags, meta descriptions, headings (e.g., H1, H2), and throughout your page content. However, be careful not to overuse them (a practice known as **keyword stuffing**), as this can harm your rankings.

Wix allows you to add keywords to the SEO settings of each page. By incorporating relevant keywords in the right places, you can significantly improve your site's visibility on search engines.

Optimizing Site Speed and Performance

Site speed is one of the most important factors in user experience and SEO. Google has made it clear that page load time is a ranking factor, and sites that load slowly are likely to rank lower in search results. Moreover, slow-loading websites lead to higher bounce rates, meaning visitors leave the site before engaging with the content.

Why Site Speed Matters

- **Search Engine Ranking**: Faster websites tend to rank higher in search engine results because they provide a better user experience.

- **User Experience**: A slow-loading site frustrates visitors and may lead them to leave before seeing your content, which can harm your site's engagement.

- **Mobile Performance**: Mobile users expect fast-loading sites. A delay of just a few seconds can result in a significant drop in traffic.

How to Optimize Site Speed on Wix

Wix provides several built-in tools to help improve your site's speed:

- **Use Optimized Images**: Large, unoptimized images can slow down your website. Use Wix's image optimization features to compress images without sacrificing quality. You can also compress images before uploading them to Wix using tools like TinyPNG.

- **Minimize the Use of Heavy Elements**: Some elements, such as large video files, sliders, or animations, can significantly affect page load times. Limit the use of these elements, and ensure that any heavy media files are optimized for faster loading.

- **Use Wix's Site Speed Settings**: Wix offers various tools to improve site speed, including **Lazy Loading**, which ensures that images and other media are only loaded when they come into the user's view. Enabling this setting will help improve page load times.

To test your site's speed, you can use tools like **Google PageSpeed Insights** or **GTmetrix**. These tools provide detailed reports on what's slowing down your site and give you actionable recommendations.

Setting Up Google Analytics and Other Tracking Tools

Tracking your website's performance is essential for understanding how users are interacting with your content and measuring the effectiveness of your SEO efforts. Wix makes it easy to integrate **Google Analytics** and other tracking tools into your site to monitor key metrics like traffic, conversions, bounce rates, and more.

Setting Up Google Analytics

1. **Create a Google Analytics Account**: If you don't already have one, go to the Google Analytics website and create an account.

2. **Get Your Tracking Code**: After setting up your account, you'll receive a **tracking ID** (a unique code).

3. **Connect Google Analytics to Wix**: In the Wix Editor, go to **Settings**, click on **Tracking & Analytics**, and then click **+ New Tool**. Paste your tracking ID into the appropriate field and save.

Once Google Analytics is connected, you'll be able to track visitor activity, behavior, and conversions on your site. You can also use the data to identify areas for improvement, such as high bounce rates or low conversion rates.

Other Tracking Tools

In addition to Google Analytics, Wix supports other tracking and marketing tools, such as:

- **Google Search Console**: Helps monitor your website's performance in search results and provides insights into how Google crawls and indexes your site.

- **Facebook Pixel**: Tracks the effectiveness of your Facebook and Instagram ads by monitoring conversions and user behavior on your site.

- **Hotjar**: This tool provides heatmaps, visitor recordings, and feedback polls to help you understand how users interact with your site.

Integrating these tools into your site allows you to collect data that will help you refine your SEO strategy and improve your site's performance.

Mobile Optimization Techniques

With the majority of internet traffic now coming from mobile devices, optimizing your website for mobile users is no longer optional—it's essential. Wix makes it easy to ensure that your site is mobile-friendly, but there are a few best practices to follow to ensure that your site looks and functions properly on mobile devices.

Wix's Mobile Editor

Wix automatically creates a mobile version of your site, but you can further customize it using the **Mobile Editor**. To access it, click on the **Mobile Icon** in the Wix Editor.

Here's what you can do in the mobile editor:

- **Rearrange Elements**: You can adjust the position and size of elements specifically for mobile devices. For example, you might want to stack images and text on mobile for a cleaner layout.

- **Hide Elements**: Some elements may look fine on desktop but clutter the mobile version of your site. You can hide certain elements on mobile, such as large images, widgets, or pop-ups that may affect load times or user experience.

- **Adjust Font Sizes**: Text might appear too small or too large on mobile devices. Use the mobile editor to adjust font sizes for better readability.

Responsive Design

Wix's templates are built with **responsive design** in mind, meaning they automatically adjust to different screen sizes. However, it's important to regularly test your site on various devices to ensure that it looks good on all screens. Use tools like Google's **Mobile-Friendly Test** to see how your site performs on mobile.

SEO and site optimization are essential components of building a successful Wix website. By using tools like

Wix's **SEO Wiz**, following best practices for on-page SEO, and optimizing your site's speed, performance, and mobile experience, you can improve your website's visibility, user experience, and overall performance. Additionally, integrating tools like **Google Analytics** and other tracking services will allow you to monitor and refine your SEO efforts, ensuring that your website ranks well and achieves its goals. By following the techniques outlined in this chapter, you'll be well on your way to creating an optimized and successful Wix website.

Chapter 8: E-Commerce with Wix: Building Your Online Store

In the digital age, the ability to run an online store has become a necessity for businesses of all sizes. Whether you're a seasoned entrepreneur or a new business owner, building an online store can significantly boost your reach, sales, and brand presence. One of the most accessible and robust tools for creating an e-commerce website is **Wix**, which offers an intuitive platform with powerful features for building and managing an online store. With Wix's **eCommerce** tools, you can set up a professional, user-friendly online shop that allows you to sell products, manage inventory, process transactions, and engage with your customers effectively.

In this chapter, we'll walk you through the process of setting up an online store using Wix eCommerce. We'll explore how to manage your products and categories, set up secure payment gateways, create promotional strategies, and handle orders, shipping, and customer service—all within the Wix platform. Whether you're selling physical products, digital downloads, or services, Wix has the tools to help you build and grow a successful online store.

Setting Up an Online Store with Wix eCommerce

Building an online store on Wix is designed to be simple and user-friendly, with no coding experience required. The platform offers a range of templates and e-commerce tools to help you create a professional-looking store. Let's walk through the key steps of setting up your store on Wix:

1. Creating an Account on Wix

Before you can start building your store, you'll need to create a Wix account. If you already have one, log in to get started. If you don't have an account yet, go to the Wix homepage and sign up using your email address or a Google or Facebook account.

2. Choosing a Template

Once you've logged into your Wix account, the next step is selecting a template for your online store. Wix offers a variety of **eCommerce templates** designed specifically for different types of businesses. Whether you're selling fashion, beauty products, electronics, or digital downloads, you'll find a template that suits your needs.

- Go to the **Wix template gallery** and select **Online Store** as the category.

- Browse through the templates and choose one that fits your business's aesthetic and functionality needs.

- Once you've selected a template, you can customize it using Wix's drag-and-drop editor to match your brand's style and goals.

3. Enabling Wix eCommerce Features

After selecting a template, you can enable Wix's **eCommerce features** to begin setting up your store. This includes adding product pages, shopping carts, payment systems, and other essential store components.

To enable Wix eCommerce:

1. In the Wix Editor, click on **Add** and select **Store**.

2. Click on **Add to Site** to activate eCommerce tools like product galleries and shopping carts.

3. Follow the prompts to start customizing your store's layout, including the **homepage**, **product pages**, and **checkout page**.

At this point, you can begin uploading your products, adding product descriptions, and organizing your store.

Managing Products, Categories, and Inventory

Managing products and inventory is one of the most crucial aspects of running an online store. Wix provides a built-in **product management system** that allows you to upload products, create categories, track inventory, and more. Let's take a closer look at how to manage these elements effectively:

1. Adding Products

To add products to your Wix store:

1. Go to the **Wix Editor** and click on **Store Products** under the **Store** section in the sidebar.

2. Click **Add New Product** to start uploading your product.

3. You will be prompted to enter the following details:

- ○ **Product Name**: Choose a name that accurately describes the product.

- ○ **Product Images**: Upload high-quality images that show off your product from multiple angles.

- ○ **Product Description**: Write a detailed description, including key features, benefits, and any other relevant information.

- ○ **Price**: Set the price for the product. You can also set sale prices or discounts.

- ○ **SKU (Stock Keeping Unit)**: Assign a unique identifier to each product for inventory management.

Wix also allows you to upload **bulk products** if you have many items to add at once. You can do this by importing a CSV file containing your product details.

2. Organizing Products into Categories

You can organize your products into categories (e.g., men's apparel, electronics, books, etc.) to make it easier for customers to find what they're looking for.

Here's how to set up product categories:

1. Go to **Store Products** in the Wix Editor.

2. Select **Categories** from the menu and click **Add New Category**.

3. Name the category and assign products to it by selecting from your product list.

You can create as many categories as needed to organize your products in a logical, user-friendly way. Categories are especially useful for larger stores with multiple product types.

3. Managing Inventory

Wix allows you to track inventory levels for each product and set alerts when stock is low. To manage your inventory:

1. When adding or editing a product, scroll down to the **Inventory** section.

2. Enable the **Track Inventory** option and enter the quantity of the product in stock.

3. You can set up **low-stock notifications** to alert you when inventory is running low so that you can reorder products in time.

You can also set the inventory to unlimited for digital products (like eBooks or downloadable music) since they don't require physical stock.

Payment Gateways and Setting Up Secure Transactions

One of the most critical aspects of running an e-commerce store is ensuring that you can process payments securely. Wix integrates with a wide variety of **payment gateways**, allowing you to accept payments from customers worldwide. Let's take a look at how to set up payment gateways and secure transactions on your Wix store.

1. Setting Up Payment Methods

Wix supports several payment options, including **credit cards**, **PayPal**, and **offline payments**. To set up payment methods:

1. In the Wix Editor, go to **Settings** and click on **Accept Payments**.

2. Select your preferred payment gateways. Wix Payments is the default option, allowing you to accept credit/debit card payments.

3. If you prefer, you can enable **PayPal** by selecting the option and linking your PayPal account.

4. If your business model allows it, you can also accept offline payments, such as cash on delivery (COD) or bank transfers.

Wix Payments offers the convenience of processing payments directly through Wix's secure platform, making it easier to manage transactions and handle customer data. However, depending on your preferences, you can also use other third-party gateways, such as Stripe or Square.

2. Enabling SSL Security

When running an eCommerce store, ensuring that your transactions are secure is paramount. Wix automatically provides an **SSL certificate** (Secure Socket Layer) for all paid plans, which encrypts customer information during transactions. This security measure ensures that sensitive data, such as credit card details, is protected.

If you're using Wix Payments or any other payment gateway, make sure to enable SSL to keep your customers' data secure.

3. Taxes and Shipping Costs

Wix also allows you to set up tax rates and shipping costs for different regions. To do this:

1. In the **Accept Payments** settings, click on **Tax** to set your region-specific tax rates.

2. In the **Shipping** section, you can specify the shipping methods you offer (e.g., free shipping, flat-rate shipping, or carrier-based shipping) and the regions you deliver to.

Make sure to set up taxes and shipping options according to the laws and regulations of the regions you serve.

Creating Promotional Codes, Discounts, and Sales Strategies

Promotions and discounts are powerful tools for driving sales and attracting customers. Wix makes it easy to create **discount codes**, **sales**, and **special**

offers to help boost your store's performance. Let's explore how you can implement these features:

1. Creating Discount Codes

To create discount codes:

1. Go to the **Wix Editor** and click on **Store > Discounts**.

2. Click on + **New Discount** to create a new offer.

3. Choose from the following discount types:

   o **Percentage Discount**: A percentage off the total order (e.g., 20% off).

   o **Fixed Amount Discount**: A fixed discount amount (e.g., $10 off).

   o **Free Shipping**: Offer free shipping for orders over a specific amount.

   o **Buy One Get One Free**: Encourage customers to buy more with "Buy One, Get One Free" deals.

Set the terms of the discount, including the validity period, usage limits, and conditions (e.g., minimum purchase amount). Once created, customers can apply the discount code at checkout.

2. Setting Up Seasonal Sales

Wix also allows you to run **seasonal sales** or **flash sales** to create a sense of urgency among your customers. To set up a sale:

1. Click on **Store** > **Sales**.

2. Choose the products you want to put on sale.

3. Set the discount amount or percentage.

4. Set the duration of the sale and any additional terms (e.g., sale limited to specific categories or regions).

Seasonal sales are a great way to clear out inventory, attract new customers, or encourage repeat business.

3. Offering Bundles or Packages

Another effective sales strategy is to create **product bundles** or **package deals**. Wix allows you to offer discounts on bundled products (e.g., a "Buy 2, Get 1 Free" offer). This strategy helps increase average order value and encourages customers to buy more.

Handling Orders, Shipping, and Customer Service

Once you've set up your online store, it's crucial to have systems in place for handling orders, shipping, and customer service. Wix offers tools to streamline these processes and ensure a positive experience for both you and your customers.

1. Managing Orders

To manage your orders:

1. Go to the **Wix Dashboard** and click on **Store Orders**.

2. Here, you'll see all customer orders, including order details, payment status, and shipping information.

3. You can mark orders as **paid**, **shipped**, or **complete**, and you can also issue refunds if necessary.

You can also **send automated order confirmation emails** to customers and set up **email notifications** for order updates.

2. Shipping Management

Wix provides tools to help you manage your store's shipping logistics:

1. Set up **shipping rules** and shipping methods for different regions.

2. Offer real-time shipping rates based on the carrier (e.g., UPS, USPS, FedEx) if you're using carrier-based shipping.

3. Track shipments directly from the Wix dashboard.

Communicate shipping times, costs, and policies clearly to your customers and provide them with tracking information once their order has been dispatched.

3. Customer Service

Providing excellent customer service is essential for building trust and ensuring customer satisfaction. Wix offers tools that allow you to engage with customers:

- **Live Chat**: You can integrate live chat functionality to answer customer queries in real time.

- **Contact Forms**: Add contact forms to your site for customers to reach out with inquiries.

- **Help Center**: Create an FAQ section to address common customer questions and reduce the volume of support requests.

Providing quick and helpful responses to customer inquiries can help build long-term customer relationships and encourage repeat business.

Building an online store with Wix eCommerce is an exciting and rewarding process that allows you to tap into the global marketplace and reach customers from all over the world. From setting up your store and managing products to creating promotional discounts and handling orders, Wix provides all the tools you need to create a successful eCommerce business. By leveraging Wix's powerful eCommerce features, payment gateways, shipping options, and customer service tools, you can build a store that not only meets your business needs but also provides a seamless and enjoyable shopping experience for your customers. With these features in place, you're well on your way to building a thriving online store.

Chapter 9: Publishing Your Website and Going Live

Once you've put in the hard work of designing, customizing, and refining your website, the final step is to make it live and accessible to the world. But before you hit the "Publish" button, it's essential to take a few key steps to ensure your site is fully functional, optimized, and ready for visitors. In this chapter, we will guide you through the process of publishing your website on Wix, previewing and testing it to ensure everything works perfectly, and understanding the differences between **previewing** and **publishing** your site. We'll also cover important aspects like **connecting a domain name**, **setting up email accounts**, and ensuring that your site has the **right hosting** to ensure fast load times and reliable performance.

By the end of this chapter, you will be ready to take your website live with confidence, knowing that it's been thoroughly tested and is fully optimized for the best possible user experience.

Previewing and Testing Your Site Before Publishing

Before publishing your website, it's crucial to ensure that everything functions properly and looks great across all devices. **Previewing** your website is a vital step in the process because it gives you a chance to experience your site from the perspective of your visitors, making sure the design, functionality, and content are in place as you intended.

Why Previewing and Testing Matter

Previewing your site ensures that it is:

- **User-Friendly**: Testing allows you to catch any usability issues that could impact visitors' interactions with your site.

- **Fully Functional**: It's important to check if all features, such as forms, buttons, and links, work properly.

- **Mobile-Optimized**: Since a significant portion of internet traffic comes from mobile devices, it's essential to check that your site is responsive and functions well on smartphones and tablets.

- **Error-Free**: Previewing gives you a final chance to fix any spelling errors, broken links, or misaligned elements that could detract from your website's professionalism.

How to Preview Your Wix Website

Wix makes it easy to preview your website before publishing it. Here's how:

1. **Open Wix Editor**: Go to the Wix Editor and ensure that you are logged into your account.

2. **Click on "Preview"**: The "Preview" button is at the top right corner of the editor. Clicking it will take you to your website's preview mode, where you can interact with it as if it were live.

3. **Test Features and Links**: While in preview mode, click through all of your pages and test all interactive elements, such as forms, buttons, and navigation links. Make sure all external links work as expected and that no pages are broken.

4. **Check Content Alignment and Design**: Examine your website's design elements. Ensure that text is properly aligned, images are

displayed correctly, and the layout looks consistent across all pages.

5. **Test Mobile View**: Since many users access websites on their mobile devices, it's essential to check how your website looks and functions on smaller screens. Wix allows you to preview the mobile version of your website directly within the editor by clicking on the **mobile icon** at the top of the editor. Ensure that elements are resized and rearranged appropriately for mobile devices.

While previewing, take notes on any adjustments you need to make and tweak the design, content, or functionality as needed. Once you're satisfied with the look and performance, you're ready to proceed with publishing.

Understanding the Differences Between Publishing and Preview Modes

Before publishing your Wix website, it's essential to understand the differences between **preview mode** and **publishing mode**. Both modes are important parts of the website creation process, but they serve different purposes.

Preview Mode

- **What It Is**: Preview mode allows you to view your website as it would appear once it's live. You can interact with the site and navigate through pages, links, forms, and buttons. However, any changes made in preview mode won't be saved permanently.

- **What You Can Do**: In preview mode, you can test all interactive elements, review your website's layout, and make sure everything looks good. You can make adjustments while previewing your site in the editor, but these changes will only take effect once you publish the site.

- **What It Isn't**: Preview mode is not the same as publishing the site. While you can see your website in a live-like environment, it's still not accessible to the public. You can make edits and preview them, but these edits won't be visible to others until the site is officially published.

Publishing Mode

- **What It Is**: Publishing mode makes your website live and accessible to the public. Once you hit the **Publish** button, your site will be available for everyone to see and interact with, as long as they have the link or search engines index it.

- **What You Can Do**: After publishing your site, visitors can access it, interact with its content, and use all the features you've set up. Your website is officially part of the online ecosystem and visible to anyone with the URL.

- **What It Isn't**: Once your site is published, you can still make changes to it. You can return to the editor to make adjustments, update content, and refine the design. However, any changes made after publishing won't be reflected on the live site until you **re-publish** it.

It's important to remember that while previewing your site gives you a sense of how it will look and function, **publishing** makes it real and accessible to the world. Therefore, always make sure to thoroughly test and preview your site before making it live.

Connecting Your Domain Name to Wix

A domain name is your website's unique address on the internet, and it's one of the most important elements of establishing your online presence. While Wix provides a **wixsite.com** subdomain for free websites, having a custom domain name (e.g., **yourbusiness.com**) adds professionalism and credibility to your website. Connecting your domain to Wix is an essential step for any serious website owner, especially for businesses, blogs, and e-commerce sites.

Why You Need a Custom Domain Name

- **Branding**: A custom domain reinforces your brand identity and helps users remember your website.

- **Credibility**: A unique domain name makes your site appear more professional and trustworthy, which is essential if you're selling products or services or building a personal brand.

- **SEO Benefits**: While a custom domain doesn't directly affect SEO rankings, it does help establish your site as a legitimate and authoritative source, which can indirectly influence search engine rankings.

How to Connect a Domain to Wix

Wix makes it easy to connect a custom domain name to your website, whether you're purchasing a new domain through Wix or transferring an existing domain from another provider. Here's how to do it:

1. Purchasing a Domain from Wix

If you haven't purchased a domain yet, Wix offers an easy domain purchasing process:

1. **Go to the Wix Dashboard**: In the Wix Editor, click on the **Settings** option in the top menu.

2. **Click on "Domains"**: From the drop-down menu, select **Domains**.

3. **Search for a Domain**: Wix will prompt you to search for available domain names. Enter your desired name and see if it's available for purchase.

4. **Purchase Your Domain**: If your chosen domain is available, you can complete the purchase directly through Wix. Wix offers

domain names with various extensions, such as .com, .net, and .org.

2. Connecting an Existing Domain to Wix

If you already own a domain through a third-party provider (e.g., GoDaddy, Namecheap, or Google Domains), you can easily connect it to your Wix site. Here's how:

1. **Go to the Wix Dashboard**: In the Wix Editor, click on **Settings** and then **Domains**.

2. **Click on "Connect a Domain You Already Own"**: Select this option to link your existing domain to Wix.

3. **Follow the Instructions**: Wix will guide you through the process of connecting your domain. You may need to log in to your domain provider's account to update your DNS settings or change your nameservers to point to Wix.

Publishing Your Site with Your Custom Domain

Once your domain is connected, click the **Publish** button. Your website will now be live and accessible via your custom domain, giving you full control over your online presence.

Setting Up Email Accounts and Ensuring Proper Hosting Setup

Once your website is live, it's important to set up **professional email accounts** that use your custom domain and ensure that your **hosting setup** is optimized for performance. Wix offers tools and integrations to help you with both.

Setting Up Email Accounts with Your Domain

Having a custom email address that matches your domain name (e.g., info@yourbusiness.com) is essential for professionalism and brand consistency. Wix integrates with **G Suite by Google** to offer business email services.

How to Set Up Email with Wix

1. **Go to Wix's Email Setup Page**: In your Wix dashboard, navigate to the **Email & G Suite** section under **Settings**.

2. **Choose a Plan**: Wix offers **G Suite by Google** for setting up business email accounts.

Select a plan that fits your needs (e.g., **Basic**, **Business**, or **Enterprise**).

3. **Complete the Setup**: Wix will guide you through linking your domain to **Google Workspace**, allowing you to set up professional email addresses and manage them through your Google account.

Once set up, you can create email addresses such as contact@yourbusiness.com, sales@yourbusiness.com, and support@yourbusiness.com.

Ensuring Proper Hosting Setup

Wix handles hosting for you automatically, so you don't have to worry about finding a third-party hosting provider. Wix's **hosting infrastructure** is fast, secure, and reliable, but there are still a few steps you can take to ensure optimal performance:

- **Enable SSL**: Wix automatically provides SSL (Secure Sockets Layer) for all paid plans, which encrypts data between your website and your visitors. This is essential for **security** and **trust**.

- **Optimize Site Speed**: Wix's hosting setup is optimized for performance, but you should also follow best practices for speed optimization, such as compressing images, using **Lazy Load** for large media, and minimizing the use of heavy elements.

- **Monitor Website Performance**: Once your site is live, use **Google PageSpeed Insights** or **GTmetrix** to monitor its performance. These tools can give you detailed reports on site speed and suggestions for further optimization.

Publishing your website on Wix and taking it live is an exciting milestone, but it's essential to ensure that every aspect of your site is ready for visitors. By previewing and testing your site thoroughly, understanding the differences between previewing and publishing, and setting up a custom domain, professional email accounts, and proper hosting, you can ensure a smooth transition to a live website. Once your site is published and accessible to the world, you can start attracting visitors, growing your audience, and working towards your business or personal goals. With these steps completed, you are now ready to enjoy the benefits of a fully operational and optimized Wix website.

Chapter 10: Maintaining and Updating Your Wix Website

Creating a stunning Wix website is just the beginning of your journey. Once your website is live, the real work begins in terms of keeping it functional, fresh, and secure. Regular maintenance and updates are essential for ensuring that your website remains user-friendly, fast, and optimized for both visitors and search engines. Whether you're running an online store, a personal blog, or a portfolio, keeping your site updated is key to maintaining a strong online presence.

In this chapter, we'll explore the best practices for maintaining and updating your Wix website. We'll discuss how to keep your content fresh and relevant, back up your website to avoid losing valuable data, monitor your website's performance, and troubleshoot common issues. By the end of this chapter, you will be equipped with the knowledge to maintain and manage your Wix website for continued success effectively.

Regular Updates and Content Management Best Practices

One of the most important aspects of maintaining your Wix website is regularly updating your content.

Keeping your content fresh not only engages your visitors but also boosts your SEO rankings, ensuring that search engines view your website as relevant and active. Here are some best practices for updating and managing your content effectively:

1. Update Content Regularly

Keeping your website's content up-to-date is essential for attracting and retaining visitors. Whether it's blog posts, product descriptions, or portfolio items, regularly adding new content ensures that your audience has something fresh to look at. For example:

- **Blog Posts**: Regularly post new articles that are relevant to your target audience. Aim to write content that addresses common questions, provides valuable insights, or showcases your expertise. Fresh blog posts signal to search engines that your site is active, which can improve your search rankings.

- **Product Listings**: If you run an online store, keep your product listings updated. Add new products, update inventory levels, and modify prices when necessary. This ensures that your online store reflects your current offerings.

- **Portfolio Updates**: If you're showcasing your work, it's important to update your portfolio with your latest projects regularly. This helps demonstrate that you're actively working and gives potential clients or employers an up-to-date view of your skills and experience.

By updating your content frequently, you not only provide fresh material for your audience but also signal to search engines that your website is relevant and frequently maintained.

2. Organize and Manage Content Effectively

Managing content on your Wix website requires careful organization. As your site grows, it can become overwhelming to manage multiple pages, blog posts, product listings, and other content. Here are a few tips to help keep your content organized:

- **Categories and Tags**: Use categories and tags to organize your content. For example, if you have a blog, create categories like "SEO Tips," "Business Advice," or "Wix Tutorials" to make it easier for visitors to find relevant articles. Tags can help break down content further and make it even more accessible.

- **Navigation Structure**: Ensure that your site's navigation remains simple and user-friendly. If you add new sections, ensure that they are logically placed in the menu so that visitors can easily find them.

- **Content Calendar**: Plan and schedule content updates ahead of time. This can help you stay organized and consistent with your content. For example, if you run a blog, create a content calendar to keep track of when you're posting new articles and to make sure you're consistently producing content.

3. Refresh Old Content

In addition to adding new content, it's also important to periodically review and refresh older content. This can be a simple update, such as adding new information, fixing broken links, or improving SEO. Google values content that is consistently updated, and refreshing old content can improve its performance in search engine results. Here are some ways to refresh your content:

- **Update Text and Information**: Ensure that all information on your website is still relevant.

For instance, if your blog posts contain outdated statistics or references, update them with the most current data.

- **SEO Optimization**: Over time, you might discover new keywords or SEO strategies that can help improve your site's performance. Regularly check and optimize your old posts with new keywords or updated meta descriptions to improve SEO.

- **Internal Linking**: Link to your newer content from older blog posts or pages. This can help increase the visibility of new content while also improving your website's overall SEO.

4. Engage with Your Audience

Maintaining engagement with your audience is also part of content management. Responding to comments, messages, and inquiries promptly helps build trust and a loyal following. If you run a blog or an e-commerce store, take the time to engage with your visitors:

- **Reply to Comments**: Responding to comments on your blog, product reviews, or social media is an effective way to keep the conversation going and demonstrate that you value your audience's input.

- **Contact Forms and Emails**: Ensure that your contact forms and email addresses are up to date. Respond to customer inquiries in a timely and professional manner.

How to Back Up Your Site and Keep It Safe

Having a backup of your website is essential in case something goes wrong. Whether your site experiences a technical issue, gets hacked, or a mistake is made during an update, a backup ensures that you can restore your site quickly and with minimal downtime. Wix makes it easy to back up your website, but it's still important to save copies of your site and its content regularly.

1. How to Back Up Your Wix Website

Wix automatically saves your site's progress and updates in real time, but it's important to back up your site manually on a regular basis. Here's how:

1. **Log into your Wix Account**: Go to your Wix dashboard and select the website you want to back up.

2. **Click on "Site History"**: In the dashboard, navigate to the **Site History** section, which provides a list of all your website's versions.

3. **Restore an Earlier Version**: If needed, you can restore an earlier version of your website by selecting the date you want to revert to. This is useful in case something goes wrong with a recent update or edit.

2. Exporting Site Data

While Wix doesn't offer a direct way to export all of your content, you can export some elements like blogs or contact lists:

- **Blog Export**: If you have a blog on Wix, you can export the blog posts as an XML file for backup.

- **Contact Database**: If you have a customer or email list, you can export it as a CSV file.

3. Downloading Your Site's Content

You can download your site's images, videos, and other files for a more comprehensive backup. While Wix doesn't allow you to download the full website as a complete package, you can download individual files to ensure that you have copies of important content, such as product images or blog images.

4. Using Third-Party Backup Tools

While Wix's built-in backup features are useful, you may want to consider using **third-party backup tools** to ensure extra security for your website. Some backup apps available in the **Wix App Market** can help automate the process of backing up your content, making it easier to restore your site in case of an emergency.

Monitoring Website Performance and Making Improvements

Monitoring the performance of your Wix website is crucial for identifying issues, understanding user behavior, and optimizing your site for better results. By tracking your website's performance, you can identify areas that need improvement, whether it's speed, SEO, or user engagement.

1. Google Analytics Integration

Google Analytics is one of the most powerful tools for monitoring website performance. It provides in-depth insights into your site's traffic, audience demographics, user behavior, and much more. Integrating Google Analytics with your Wix site is simple:

1. **Sign Up for Google Analytics**: If you haven't already, sign up for a Google Analytics account at analytics.google.com.

2. **Get Your Tracking Code**: Once you've signed up, Google Analytics will provide you with a unique tracking ID.

3. **Add the Tracking Code to Wix**: In the Wix Editor, go to **Settings** > **Tracking & Analytics**. Click on **+ New Tool** and paste your Google Analytics tracking code into the provided field.

Once connected, you can start tracking key metrics such as:

- **Traffic**: See how many visitors are coming to your site, where they're coming from, and what pages they're visiting.

- **Bounce Rate**: Track how many users leave your site after viewing only one page. A high bounce rate may indicate issues with your content or user experience.

- **Conversion Tracking**: Set up goals and track conversions, such as form submissions, purchases, or newsletter sign-ups.

2. Wix Site Performance Tools

Wix offers several built-in tools to help you monitor and optimize your website's performance:

- **Site Speed**: Wix's **Site Speed** tool allows you to check how quickly your website loads. Slow load times can negatively impact both user experience and SEO rankings. You can use this tool to identify areas for improvement, such as large image files, videos, or heavy elements that may be slowing down your site.

- **SEO Tools**: Wix's **SEO Wiz** tool helps you optimize your site for search engines by providing personalized recommendations. You can monitor your SEO progress and make necessary adjustments to improve your rankings.

- **Mobile Optimization**: Since a significant portion of web traffic comes from mobile devices, it's essential to monitor how your website performs on mobile. Use Wix's mobile editor to ensure that your site is responsive and optimized for mobile users.

3. Testing Website Functionality

Regular testing is essential for ensuring that everything on your site works

as it should. This includes:

- **Testing Forms**: Ensure that all forms (contact forms, registration forms, etc.) are working correctly. Test them regularly to ensure that data is being submitted and stored correctly.

- **Broken Links**: Use tools like **Dead Link Checker** to identify and fix any broken links on your website. Broken links can harm both your user experience and SEO rankings.

Troubleshooting Common Wix Website Issues

Even after creating a beautiful website, you may encounter issues that need to be resolved. Common problems can include broken links, slow loading times, or issues with site elements not displaying correctly. Here are a few troubleshooting tips to help you address common Wix website issues:

1. Site Speed Issues

If your site is loading slowly, here are a few potential causes and solutions:

- **Heavy Images**: Large image files can significantly slow down your site. Compress images before uploading them to Wix or use Wix's built-in image optimization tools.

- **Too Many Apps**: While apps can add useful functionality, too many can slow down your site. Remove unnecessary apps from your Wix site and keep only those that are essential.

- **Excessive Animations**: While animations can make your site more dynamic, too many animations can negatively affect loading times. Consider reducing the number of animations, especially on important pages.

2. Content Display Issues

If elements on your site are not displaying correctly (such as text or images), try these solutions:

- **Check Browser Compatibility**: Ensure that your website is compatible with all major browsers, including Chrome, Firefox, Safari, and Edge. Test your site on different browsers to identify compatibility issues.

- **Clear Cache**: Sometimes, outdated content may appear in the browser cache. Clearing your browser's cache can help resolve this issue.

- **Responsive Design**: Ensure that your site is optimized for desktop and mobile devices. If certain elements do not appear correctly on mobile, adjust them using the mobile editor in Wix.

3. Fixing Broken Links

Broken links are common issues that can hurt your site's performance and SEO. Use tools like **Dead Link Checker** or the built-in **Wix Site Analysis** tool to identify and fix broken links on your website.

Maintaining and updating your Wix website is crucial to ensuring that it remains functional, relevant, and optimized for both visitors and search engines. By regularly updating your content, backing up your site, monitoring performance, and troubleshooting common issues, you can keep your website running smoothly and successfully. With the right tools and strategies in place, your Wix website will continue to grow and thrive in the competitive online landscape.

Wix Website

Chapter 11: Future-Proofing Your Wix Website

Building a successful website is an ongoing process. The work doesn't end when you launch your site; it's important to continuously adapt and evolve your website as your business, project, or personal brand grows. This concept is known as **future-proofing**, and it involves making strategic decisions and using the right tools to ensure your site remains relevant, functional, and scalable as your needs change over time. Whether you're growing an online business, a personal blog, or a portfolio, future-proofing your Wix website can help you stay ahead of the curve and continue to meet the demands of your audience.

In this chapter, we will explore the importance of future-proofing your Wix website, focusing on how to **adapt your site as your business grows**, **scale your website** when you need more features or performance, and anticipate the **future of Wix** and its evolving tools. We will also discuss the wealth of **community resources**, such as Wix forums, blogs, and support channels, that can assist you in your journey of continuous improvement.

Adapting Your Site as Your Business or Project Grows

As your business or project evolves, so should your website. The key to future-proofing is understanding that your website should be adaptable to change, whether you're expanding your product offerings, changing your branding, or adding new services. Below are several ways you can adapt your Wix site to grow with your business or personal brand.

1. Expanding Your Product or Service Offerings

As your business grows, you may find that your product or service offerings expand. This means your website will need to accommodate these new offerings. Wix's **eCommerce** features allow you to add new products or services easily, whether you're expanding your inventory, introducing new categories, or offering a new product line.

- **Add New Products**: Use Wix's product management tools to add new products to your online store quickly. Create clear, descriptive product pages and update your **product categories** and **inventory management** settings to reflect the new items.

- **Create New Service Pages**: If your business is service-oriented, you can easily add new service pages to your site. Ensure that each service has its dedicated page with clear descriptions, pricing, and images to help potential customers better understand what you offer.

2. Changing or Updating Your Brand Identity

As your business or project evolves, so may your branding. Whether you're updating your logo, changing your color scheme, or revising your messaging, Wix makes it easy to change your site's appearance and messaging to reflect these changes.

- **Update Your Design**: Wix offers a wide variety of customizable templates that make it simple to refresh your website's design. You can adjust your site's **fonts**, **colors**, **backgrounds**, and **layout** to match your new branding.

- **Rebrand Your Content**: If your brand messaging has changed, it's important to revise your website's content as well. Update key pages, such as the **About Us** page, **Home**

Page, and product/service descriptions, to reflect your new voice and values.

Changing your branding is a crucial step in business growth, and Wix's flexible tools make it easy to adapt your website to these changes.

3. Adding New Functionalities and Features

As your business grows, you may need to add new features or functionalities to your website. Wix offers a variety of built-in features, apps, and integrations that can help you add new capabilities to your site without writing any code.

- **Wix App Market**: The Wix App Market is home to hundreds of apps that can enhance your site's functionality. If you need to add a booking system, live chat, email marketing tools, or social media integration, you can find apps that suit your needs. Browse the market and install the apps that will help you grow.

- **Custom Code with Wix Velo**: For more advanced users, Wix Velo allows you to write custom JavaScript code to add unique features to your website. This could include interactive elements, dynamic content, or custom databases. Velo enables you to scale your website by integrating third-party APIs and services that may be necessary as your business grows.

Adding new features as your business evolves ensures that your website continues to meet your customers' needs and keep up with the competition.

Scaling Your Website: What to Do When You Need More Features or Performance

At some point, you may find that your Wix website's performance needs to be scaled to accommodate increased traffic, additional content, or more complex features. Scaling your site ensures that it continues to function smoothly as you grow. Here are several steps to take when you need to scale your website:

1. Upgrading Your Wix Plan

Wix offers several subscription plans, each designed for different levels of functionality. As your website grows, you may find that you need more features, storage, or bandwidth to support the increased demand. Wix offers **Premium Plans** that unlock additional features and improve performance.

- **Increased Storage and Bandwidth**: If you're adding more content, such as product images, blog posts, or videos, you may need more storage. Upgrading to a higher-tier plan will give you more storage and bandwidth to accommodate larger files and higher traffic volumes.

- **Advanced Features**: Some Wix Premium Plans provide access to advanced features, such as **Google Analytics integration**, **professional email accounts**, and **advanced SEO tools**, which can help optimize your site as it scales.

Upgrading your Wix plan ensures that your website has the resources it needs to handle increased traffic and more complex content.

2. Optimizing Site Performance

As your website grows, performance can become a concern, particularly if you have a lot of content or media files. Slow-loading websites can result in high bounce rates and a poor user experience. Wix provides several tools to help you optimize your site's speed and performance.

- **Image Optimization**: Ensure that your images are properly optimized for the web. Large image files can significantly slow down your site, so use Wix's image compression tools to reduce file size without sacrificing quality. You can also enable **Lazy Loading**, which ensures that images load only when they're visible to the user.

- **Remove Unnecessary Apps**: As your website grows, you may install various apps to add functionality. However, having too many apps can negatively impact performance. Regularly review your apps and remove any that are not essential to your site's function.

- **Content Delivery Network (CDN)**: Wix's built-in CDN ensures that your content is served to users quickly, regardless of their location. This speeds up page loading times, especially for international visitors.

By keeping your site optimized, you can ensure that it remains fast and functional, even as you scale.

3. Using Custom Solutions for Advanced Needs

As your site becomes more complex, you may need custom solutions to handle specific features or workflows. Wix Velo, the development platform within Wix, enables you to create custom databases, dynamic content, and third-party integrations to meet your business's unique needs.

- **Create Custom Databases**: If you need to manage large amounts of data, such as a catalog of products, customer information, or blog posts, Wix Velo allows you to create custom databases to store and manage that data. This makes it easier to keep your website organized and efficient as you scale.

- **Third-Party Integrations**: Wix Velo also enables you to integrate external APIs and services, which can enhance your site's functionality. For example, you can integrate shipping providers, payment gateways, or customer service tools to streamline operations.

As your business grows, Wix's scalability features, such as Velo and third-party integrations, will allow you to meet your website's increasing demands.

The Future of Wix: What New Features to Expect

Wix is constantly evolving to keep up with the latest trends in web design, technology, and user experience. The platform is known for its commitment to providing a powerful, intuitive experience for both beginners and advanced users. As Wix continues to develop, there are several exciting features and improvements to look forward to.

1. Enhanced AI Features

Wix has already integrated Artificial Intelligence (AI) into its platform with tools like **Wix ADI** (Artificial Design Intelligence), which automatically creates a website for users based on their preferences and needs. In the future, we can expect even more advanced AI-driven features that will help you build and manage your site more efficiently.

- **AI-Powered Content Creation**: Wix may introduce AI-powered tools that help create content for your website, such as blog posts, product descriptions, or social media captions. These tools could help save time and ensure that your content is both optimized and engaging.

- **Personalized User Experience**: Wix's AI may also be used to provide a more personalized experience for your site's visitors. For example, AI could recommend products or content based on user behavior, increasing engagement and conversions.

2. Improved SEO Tools

Search engine optimization (SEO) is essential for driving traffic to your website. Wix's SEO tools have already been helpful in guiding users through the optimization process, but there are always new developments in SEO strategies and best practices. Wix is likely to continue improving its SEO tools to make it even easier for users to improve their rankings and visibility.

- **Automated SEO Suggestions**: Wix may introduce more automated SEO suggestions based on the latest algorithm updates from Google and other search engines. This will help ensure that your site is always optimized for the best possible rankings.

- **Enhanced Analytics**: Wix could further enhance its SEO analytics tools, providing more detailed insights into how your website is performing in search results, helping you make data-driven decisions to improve your rankings.

3. Continued eCommerce Enhancements

As the e-commerce industry continues to grow, Wix will likely continue to enhance its e-commerce features to support businesses of all sizes. New features may include:

- **Advanced Payment Options**: Expect to see additional payment gateways and payment methods to accommodate customers from around the world.

- **Improved Shipping Tools**: Wix may integrate more advanced shipping features, allowing you to offer real-time shipping rates, manage international shipping, and automate fulfillment processes.

The future of Wix's eCommerce platform looks bright, with ongoing improvements to help you scale your online store.

Community Resources: Wix Forums, Blogs, and Support

As you build and grow your Wix website, it's helpful to have a community of like-minded users and resources to turn to for guidance and support. Wix offers a variety of community resources, including forums, blogs, and customer support, to help you solve problems, get advice, and learn new techniques.

1. Wix Forum

The **Wix Forum** is a great place to connect with other Wix users, share ideas, and ask questions. Whether you're seeking advice on design, e-commerce, or troubleshooting, the Wix community is a valuable resource for finding solutions and connecting with others who are facing similar challenges.

2. Wix Blog

The **Wix Blog** is regularly updated with helpful articles, tutorials, and industry insights. Whether you're looking to improve your site's SEO, learn about new Wix features, or get tips on digital marketing, the Wix Blog provides valuable information to help you succeed.

3. Wix Support

Wix also offers excellent customer support, with a range of help options including:

- **Wix Help Center**: Access detailed articles and tutorials on everything from design to SEO to troubleshooting.

- **Live Chat and Email Support**: If you have a question or encounter an issue, Wix's support team can assist you via live chat or email.

The resources available through Wix will help you stay informed, troubleshoot issues, and ensure that your website continues to perform at its best.

Future-proofing your Wix website is essential for ensuring its continued success as your business or project grows. By adapting your site, scaling it with new features, and staying informed about the latest developments, you can create a website that remains relevant, functional, and efficient. Wix's continuous innovation and extensive community resources will help you stay ahead of the curve and keep your site running smoothly. With the right tools, strategies, and support, your Wix website will continue to thrive as you move forward.

Conclusion

Building a website on Wix can be an exciting, empowering, and rewarding experience, whether you're a complete beginner or an experienced pro looking to create something new. With its user-friendly drag-and-drop editor, powerful design features, and vast array of customization options, Wix provides a platform that meets the needs of all users, no matter their level of technical expertise. Throughout this journey, we've covered a wide range of topics that will help you design, publish, and maintain your Wix website. This concluding chapter will summarize the key takeaways for both beginners and advanced users, offer some final encouragement to get started, and provide tips for continued learning and experimentation.

Recap of Key Takeaways for Both Pros and Beginners

Throughout this guide, we have delved into various aspects of using Wix, from the basics of getting started with the platform to more advanced features like eCommerce and custom coding with Wix Velo. Here's a recap of the key points for both **beginners** and **advanced users** to remember:

For Beginners:

1. **Getting Started**: Wix's drag-and-drop interface makes it easy to build a website without any coding knowledge. The first step is to choose a template that suits your style or business needs. Once you've selected your template, you can customize it by adding text, images, and elements to your page.

2. **Using Wix's SEO Tools**: Understanding the basics of SEO is crucial, even for beginners. Wix's **SEO Wiz** tool provides step-by-step guidance for optimizing your website. By following the suggestions in the tool, you can increase your site's visibility on search engines like Google.

3. **E-Commerce**: If you're building an online store, Wix makes it easy to set up product pages, organize your inventory, and process payments securely. Beginners can easily start an online business using Wix's eCommerce features without needing technical skills.

4. **Mobile Optimization**: Wix offers an automatic mobile view of your site, but it's

important to check how your site looks and functions on mobile devices. Using the mobile editor, you can ensure that your site is fully responsive and user-friendly for visitors on smartphones and tablets.

5. **Customer Support and Resources**: Wix offers a wealth of support resources for beginners. The **Wix Help Center**, tutorials, forums, and live chat provide excellent guidance when you encounter challenges. Don't hesitate to reach out and learn from the Wix community.

For Advanced Users/Pros:

1. **Customizing with Wix Velo**: For those with coding experience or those who want to take their websites to the next level, **Wix Velo** offers full control over custom features. Using JavaScript, APIs, and databases, pros can create dynamic, data-driven websites and even build complex custom applications within the Wix platform.

2. **Scaling Your Site**: As your business or project grows, your website needs to scale accordingly. Wix makes it easy to upgrade your plan for more

storage, bandwidth, and advanced features. Additionally, by adding custom functionality or integrating third-party apps, advanced users can optimize the site for performance and user experience.

3. **Advanced SEO and Marketing Tools**: Pros can dive deeper into SEO by utilizing Wix's advanced features, such as **Google Analytics** integration, custom metadata, and more sophisticated keyword strategies. Additionally, Wix's **email marketing tools** and **automated social media sharing** can help you extend your reach and drive traffic to your site.

4. **Third-Party Integrations**: Advanced users will benefit from integrating **external tools and services** like payment processors, marketing platforms, shipping solutions, and analytics tools. Wix's ability to integrate with a wide variety of third-party apps enhances the functionality of your website and streamlines your workflow.

5. **Security and Backups**: Ensuring the security and backup of your professional website is paramount. Wix offers **SSL certificates** and **site history backups** to keep your website secure and protect your data from unexpected issues or mistakes.

Common Takeaways for All Users:

- **Mobile-First Design**: Whether you're a beginner or a pro, always think about the mobile experience. Wix automatically optimizes sites for mobile, but be sure to test and customize your mobile version to ensure that your visitors have a smooth browsing experience, no matter what device they're using.

- **Content Updates and Engagement**: Websites are dynamic and require regular updates. Whether you're adding blog posts, new products, or updating services, keeping your content fresh helps keep your audience engaged and boosts your SEO.

- **Community Support**: Wix has a vibrant community of users, designers, and developers who share tips, insights, and solutions in **Wix**

forums and **social media groups**. Tap into this resource to learn from others' experiences and get help when needed.

Encouragement for Readers to Start Creating and Customizing Their Wix Websites

If you've made it this far in the guide, you've likely gained a deeper understanding of the tools and features that Wix offers. Now, it's time to take the plunge and start building or customizing your website. Whether you're creating a personal blog, a portfolio to showcase your work, or an online store, the best way to learn and grow is by diving into the process and experimenting with what Wix has to offer.

Why You Should Start Now:

- **Ease of Use**: Wix is one of the most user-friendly website builders on the market, meaning you can get started quickly without needing to learn complicated coding or design techniques.

- **Flexibility**: The platform's flexibility allows you to build any website you envision, whether it's a simple blog, a business site, or an extensive eCommerce platform. You can always start small and scale your site as your needs evolve.

- **Creative Freedom**: Wix gives you the creative freedom to express your ideas visually and functionally. Whether it's through customizable templates, apps, or custom coding, Wix gives you the tools to make your website truly yours.

- **Comprehensive Resources**: Wix offers comprehensive resources, including tutorials, FAQs, and support centers, so even beginners can feel confident in building and maintaining their websites. Advanced users also benefit from Wix's Developer Tools for even more customization.

Take the First Step:

- **Start with a Template**: If you're a beginner, start by choosing a template that fits your vision. You don't need to worry about designing from scratch; customize the template to reflect your unique style.

- **Experiment with Features**: Try experimenting with different tools and features to see how they work. Don't be afraid to make mistakes, as Wix offers an easy way to undo changes and test out new ideas.

- **Seek Inspiration**: Browse through the Wix template gallery or visit other Wix websites for inspiration. Don't be afraid to draw ideas from others, but always aim to add your personal touch and style to your site.

- **Start Small and Grow**: You don't need to launch a fully polished site right away. Start small with the basics—creating a homepage, adding some text and images—and build from there. Over time, you can refine and expand your website as your goals evolve.

Final Tips for Ongoing Learning and Experimenting with Wix Tools

Creating and maintaining a Wix website is not a one-time task. To keep your site running smoothly and effectively, it's essential to continue learning, experimenting, and adapting to new trends and features. Here are some final tips for ongoing learning and experimentation with Wix tools:

1. Keep Learning and Stay Updated

Wix is constantly updating and improving its platform. To keep up with new features, follow the **Wix Blog** and **Wix YouTube Channel** for tutorials, updates, and industry news. Regularly check out new blog posts, product releases, and webinars to stay informed about the latest tools and trends.

- **Wix Blog**: Subscribe to the official Wix Blog to get tips, inspiration, and advice on topics like SEO, eCommerce, and design.

- **Wix YouTube Channel**: Wix's YouTube channel provides tutorials and videos that guide you through specific tasks, helping you get the most out of the platform.

2. Join the Wix Community

There's a huge Wix community of designers, developers, and creators who share tips, solutions, and inspiration. Joining Wix forums and **Facebook Groups** can give you access to helpful discussions and advice from other users. You can learn new tricks, ask questions, and get feedback on your site.

- **Wix Forum**: Engage with other Wix users and ask questions in the official Wix Forum. It's a great place to connect with people who have similar experiences and challenges.

- **Wix Facebook Groups**: There are many Wix-focused groups on social media platforms like Facebook where users share tips and success stories. These groups are perfect for gaining inspiration and learning from others' experiences.

3. Experiment and Test New Features

Don't be afraid to experiment with new tools and features. Wix allows you to add or remove features with ease, so if you want to try something new, go ahead and test it on your site. Whether it's experimenting with new apps from the **Wix App Market**, integrating third-party services, or testing custom code using **Velo**, you can always make changes to improve your site's performance and functionality.

4. Optimize Regularly

Keep optimizing your site for better performance. Use Wix's **Site Speed** tool to check your page load times, and follow the SEO guidelines provided by **Wix SEO Wiz** to improve your Google rankings. Regular optimization ensures that your website is always performing at its best.

- **SEO Best Practices**: Regularly review and update your SEO settings, such as keywords, meta tags, and descriptions, to ensure your site remains relevant to search engines.

- **Content Quality**: Always aim to produce high-quality content that resonates with your audience. This can include blog posts, videos, images, and product descriptions.

5. Focus on User Experience (UX)

No matter how beautiful your website looks, the most important thing is how users experience it. Regularly check for broken links, slow loading times, and difficult navigation. Ensure that your site is user-friendly, intuitive, and easy to navigate.

- **Test User Journeys**: Regularly test the experience of navigating your website from the perspective of different users. This will help you identify areas that need improvement and ensure that your site is easy to use for everyone.

In conclusion, Wix is a versatile and powerful platform that can help you create a website tailored to your specific needs, whether you're a beginner or an advanced user. By following the tips and techniques outlined in this guide, you can confidently build and maintain a website that meets your goals and grows with your business or project.

Start creating, experimenting, and learning today. Whether you're building a personal blog, an online store, or a portfolio, Wix provides the tools, resources, and community to support you. By staying informed, continuing to optimize your site, and experimenting with new features, you can future-proof your website and ensure its long-term success. The sky's the limit—so let your creativity flow and build something amazing!